English

An Essential Grammar

This is a concise and user-friendly guide to the grammar of modern English, written specifically for native speakers.

You do not need to have studied English grammar before: all the essentials are explained here clearly and without the use of jargon. Beginning with the basics, the author then introduces more advanced topics.

Based on genuine samples of contemporary spoken and written English, the *Grammar* focuses on both British and American usage, and explores the differences – and similarities – between the two.

Features include:

- discussion of points which often cause problems
- guidance on sentence building and composition
- practical spelling rules
- explanation of grammatical terms
- appendix of irregular verbs.

English: An Essential Grammar will help you read, speak and write English with greater confidence. It is ideal for everyone who would like to improve their knowledge of English grammar.

Gerald Nelson is Research Assistant Professor in the English Department at The University of Hong Kong, and formerly Senior Research Fellow at the Survey of English Usage, University College London.

English

An Essential Grammar

 **Gerald Nelson**

London and New York

3/26/07
ww
$ 34.95

First published 2001
by Routledge
11 New Fetter Lane, London EC4P 4EE

Simultaneously published in the USA and Canada
by Routledge
29 West 35th Street, New York, NY 10001

Routledge is an imprint of the Taylor & Francis Group

Designed and Typeset in Sabon and Gill
by Florence Production Ltd, Stoodleigh, Devon

Printed and bound in Great Britain
by TJ International, Padstow, Cornwall

British Library Cataloguing in Publication Data
A catalogue record for this book is available from the British Library.

Library of Congress Cataloging-in-Publication Data
Nelson Gerald, 1959–
   English: an essential grammar / Gerald Nelson
     p. cm. – (Routledge grammars)
   Includes bibliographical references and index.
   1. English language—Grammar. I. Title: English—an essential
grammar. II. Title. III. Series
   PE1112.N45 2001
   428.2–dc21   00–045736

ISBN 0–415–22449–7 (hbk)
ISBN 0–415–22450–0 (pbk)

Contents

Introduction 1

Chapter 1 The elements of a simple sentence 9

1.1 Simple, compound, and complex sentences 9
1.2 Subject and predicate 10
1.3 Identifying the subject 11
1.4 Verb types 12
    1.4.1 Intransitive verbs *12*
    1.4.2 Linking verbs *13*
    1.4.3 Transitive verbs *14*
1.5 Subject complement 15
1.6 Direct object 16
1.7 Indirect object 17
1.8 Object complement 18
1.9 The five sentence patterns 19
1.10 Active and passive sentences 21
1.11 Adjuncts 22
1.12 The meanings of adjuncts 23
1.13 Vocatives 24
1.14 Sentence types 25
    1.14.1 Declarative sentences *25*
    1.14.2 Interrogative sentences *25*
    1.14.3 Imperative sentences *26*
    1.14.4 Exclamative sentences *27*
1.15 Fragments and non-sentences 27

Chapter 2   Words and word classes   **30**

2.1   Open and closed word classes   30

2.2   Nouns   32

     2.2.1   Singular and plural nouns   *32*

     2.2.2   Common and proper nouns   *34*

     2.2.3   Countable and uncountable nouns   *35*

     2.2.4   Genitive nouns   *36*

     2.2.5   Dependent and independent genitives   *37*

     2.2.6   The gender of nouns   *38*

2.3   Main verbs   39

     2.3.1   The five verb forms   *39*

     2.3.2   The base form   *40*

     2.3.3   The *-s* form   *41*

     2.3.4   The past form   *41*

     2.3.5   The *-ed* form   *42*

     2.3.6   The *-ing* form   *43*

     2.3.7   Irregular verbs   *43*

     2.3.8   Regular and irregular variants   *45*

     2.3.9   The verb *be*   *46*

     2.3.10   Multi-word verbs   *47*

2.4   Adjectives   48

     2.4.1   Gradable adjectives   *49*

     2.4.2   Comparative and superlative adjectives   *50*

     2.4.3   Participial adjectives   *52*

2.5   Adverbs   53

     2.5.1   Gradable adverbs   *54*

     2.5.2   Comparative and superlative adverbs   *55*

     2.5.3   Intensifiers   *55*

     2.5.4   The meanings of adverbs   *56*

2.6   Pronouns   57

     2.6.1   Personal pronouns   *57*

     2.6.2   Possessive pronouns   *60*

     2.6.3   Reflexive pronouns   *62*

     2.6.4   Gender-neutral pronouns   *62*

     2.6.5   Demonstrative pronouns   *63*

     2.6.6   Relative pronouns   *64*

     2.6.7   Pronoun *it*   *65*

     2.6.8   Pronoun *one*   *66*

2.7   Auxiliary verbs   67
        2.7.1   Modal auxiliaries   68
        2.7.2   The meanings of modal auxiliaries   69
        2.7.3   The passive auxiliary *be*   70
        2.7.4   The progressive auxiliary *be*   70
        2.7.5   The perfective auxiliary *have*   70
        2.7.6   Auxiliary *do*   71
        2.7.7   Semi-auxiliaries   72
2.8   Prepositions   72
2.9   Conjunctions   73
2.10   Articles   75
2.11   Numerals   76

Chapter 3   Phrases   **78**

3.1   The five phrase types   78
3.2   Noun phrases   79
        3.2.1   Determiners   *80*
        3.2.2   Premodifiers   *82*
        3.2.3   Postmodifiers   *83*
        3.2.4   Restrictive and non-restrictive postmodifiers   *84*
        3.2.5   Postmodifiers and complements   *84*
        3.2.6   Apposition   *85*
        3.2.7   The functions of noun phrases   *86*
3.3   Verb phrases   88
        3.3.1   The ordering of auxiliary verbs   *88*
        3.3.2   Tense   *89*
        3.3.3   Expressing future time   *90*
        3.3.4   Finite and non-finite verb phrases   *91*
        3.3.5   Aspect   *92*
        3.3.6   Mood   *93*
3.4   Adjective phrases   95
        3.4.1   The functions of adjective phrases   *96*
3.5   Adverb phrases   97
        3.5.1   The functions of adverb phrases   *97*
3.6   Prepositional phrases   98
        3.6.1   The functions of prepositional phrases   *99*

Chapter 4   Sentences and clauses   101

4.1	Complex sentences	101
4.2	Markers of subordination	102
4.3	Subordinate clause types	104

    4.3.1   Adjunct clauses   *104*
    4.3.2   Relative clauses   *105*
    4.3.3   Nominal relative clauses   *105*
    4.3.4   *That*-clauses   *106*
    4.3.5   Comparative clauses   *107*

4.4	Clauses as sentence elements	107
4.5	Clauses as phrase elements	108
4.6	The meanings of adjunct clauses	109
4.7	Peripheral clauses	110

    4.7.1   Comment clauses   *111*
    4.7.2   Reporting clauses and direct speech   *111*
    4.7.3   Tag questions   *112*
    4.7.4   Parentheticals   *112*
    4.7.5   Sentential relative clauses   *113*

4.8	Coordination	113
4.9	Coordination types	114
4.10	Pseudo-coordination	115
4.11	Sentence connectors	116

    4.11.1   Logical connectors   *116*
    4.11.2   Structural connectors   *117*

4.12	Expressing point of view	119
4.13	Referring expressions	120
4.14	Antecedent agreement	121
4.15	Substitution using *so* and *do*	122
4.16	Fronting	123
4.17	Cleft sentences	124
4.18	Postponed subjects	125
4.19	*There*-sentences	126

Chapter 5   Word formation and spelling   127

5.1	The structure of words	127
5.2	Prefixes	127
5.3	Suffixes	129
5.4	Compounding and blending	130
5.5	Acronyms, abbreviations, and clipping	133

5.6   Back formations   135
5.7   Combining forms   136
5.8   Inflections   137
5.9   Adding inflections: general spelling rules   138
5.10   Adding -*ly* and -*ally*   142
5.11   Plural nouns   143
5.12   Variants with *s* or *z*   145
5.13   British and American spelling variants   146
5.14   Problem spellings   147

Appendix: English irregular verbs   **150**

Glossary of terms   **158**

Further reading   **173**

Index   **174**

Introduction

Grammar is the study of how words combine to form sentences. The following is a well-formed, 'grammatical' sentence:

[1]   John has been ill.

Speakers of English can produce and understand a sentence like this without ever thinking about its grammar. Conversely, no speaker of English would ever produce a sentence like this:

[2]   *Ill John been has.

This is an ill-formed, 'ungrammatical' sentence. But can you say why?

The study of grammar provides us with the terminology we need to talk about language in an informed way. It enables us to analyse and to describe our own use of language, as well as that of other people. In writing, a knowledge of grammar enables us to evaluate the choices that are available to us during composition.

Grammar rules

Many people think of English grammar in terms of traditional rules, such as Never split an infinitive; Never end a sentence with a preposition. Specifically, these are **prescriptive** rules. They tell us nothing about how English is really used in everyday life. In fact, native speakers of English regularly split infinitives (to *actually consider*) and sentences often end with a preposition (*Dr Brown is the man I'll vote for.*).

---

[1] An asterisk is used throughout this book to indicate ungrammatical or incorrect examples, which are used to illustrate a point.

Prescriptive grammar reached its peak in the nineteenth century. In the twenty-first century, grammarians adopt a more **descriptive** approach. In the descriptive approach, the rules of grammar – the ones that concern us in this book – are the rules that we òbey every time we speak, even if we are completely unaware of what they are. For instance, when we say *John has been ill*, we obey many grammar rules, including rules about:

1   Where to place the subject *John* – before the verb
     (▶see 1.2)

2   Subject–verb agreement – *John has*, not *John have*
     (▶see 1.3)

3   Verb forms – *been*, not *being* (▶see 2.3.1)

These are descriptive rules. The task of the modern grammarian is to discover and then to describe the rules by which a language actually works. In order to do this, grammarians now use computer technology to help them analyse very large collections of naturally occurring language, taken from a wide variety of sources, including conversations, lectures, broadcasts, newspapers, magazines, letters and books.

Standard English

Standard English is the variety of English which carries the greatest social prestige in a speech community. In Britain, there is a standard British English, in the United States, there is a standard American English, in Australia, a standard Australian English, and so on. In each country, the national standard is that variety which is used in public institutions, including government, education, the judiciary and the media. It is used on national television and radio, and in newspapers, books and magazines. The standard variety is the only variety which has a standardized spelling. As a result, the national standard has the widest currency as a means of communication, in contrast with regional varieties, which have a more limited currency.

The following sentence is an example of standard English:

I *was* ill last week.

The following sentence is non-standard:

I were ill last week.

The non-standard past-tense construction *I were* is commonly used in several regional varieties, especially in parts of England. Regional varieties are associated with particular regions. The standard variety is not geographically bound in the same way.

Using standard English involves making choices of grammar, vocabulary and spelling. It has nothing to do with accent. The sentence *I was ill last week* is standard English whether it is spoken with a Birmingham accent, a Glasgow accent, a Cockney accent, a Newcastle accent, or any other of the many accents in Britain today. Similarly, standard American English (sometimes called 'General American') is used throughout the United States, from San Francisco to New York, from New Orleans to the Great Lakes. In both countries, the standard variety co-exists with a very large number of regional varieties. In fact, most educated people use both their own regional variety and the standard variety, and they can switch effortlessly between the two. They speak both varieties with the same accent.

No variety of English – including standard English – is inherently better or worse than any other. However, the standard variety is the one that has the greatest value in social terms as a means of communication, especially for public and professional communication. The notion of standard English is especially important to learners of the language. Because of its high social value, learners are justifiably anxious to ensure that the English they learn is standard English.

English as a world language

Conservative estimates put the total number of English speakers throughout the world at around 800 million. English is the mother tongue of an estimated 350 million people in the countries listed overleaf.

In addition to these countries, English is an official language, or has special status, in over sixty countries worldwide, including Cameroon, Ghana, India, Jamaica, Kenya, Nigeria, Tanzania, Pakistan, the Philippines and Singapore. This means that English is used in these countries in many public functions, including government, the judiciary, the press and broadcasting. Even in countries where it has no official status, such as China

Approximate number of mother-tongue English speakers, in millions	
United States	216
Great Britain	53
Canada	17
Australia	14
New Zealand	4
Ireland	3.5
South Africa	2

and Japan, English has a central place in school curricula, because its value in international communication and trade is unquestioned.

The spread of English around the world was one of the most significant linguistic developments of the twentieth century. That century also witnessed another important development: the decline of British English and the rise of American English as the dominant variety.

British English and American English

Linguistic influence follows closely on political and economic influence. For several centuries, British English was the dominant variety throughout the world, because Britain was the centre of a vast empire that straddled the globe. In the twentieth century, political power shifted dramatically away from Britain, and the United States is now both politically and economically the most powerful country in the world. It is not surprising then that American English has become the dominant variety, although the traditional influence of British English remains strong. In recent years, the worldwide influence of American English has been greatly strengthened by the mass media and the entertainment industry. American news channels such as CNN and NBC are transmitted around the world by satellite, and American films and television shows are seen on every continent. The language of the Internet is overwhelmingly American English.

The differences between American English and British English are for the most part fairly superficial. Perhaps the most familiar differences are in vocabulary:

British English	American English
autumn	fall
film	movie
flat	apartment
holiday	vacation
lift	elevator
nappy	diaper
number plate	license plate
petrol	gas
post code	zip code
rubbish	trash
shop	store
tap	faucet
taxi	cab
trainers	sneakers

Some of the American English words on this list – particularly *apartment*, *cab* and *store* – are slowly being assimilated into British English. No doubt this trend will continue. International communication and travel tend to smooth the differences between national varieties, in favour of the dominant variety.

In the spoken language, there are very noticeable differences in stress between American English and British English. For instance, American speakers generally stress the final syllable in *adult*, while British speakers stress the first syllable: *adult*. Other stress differences include:

British English	American English
ad*dress*	*add*ress
*ball*et	ball*et*
cig*arette*	*cig*arette
*deb*ris	deb*ris*
*gar*age	gar*age*
la*bor*atory	*lab*oratory
maga*zine*	*mag*azine

Finally, spelling differences include:

British English	American English
cheque	check
humour	humor
pyjamas	pajamas
theatre	theater
tyre	tire

For more on spelling differences, ▶see **5.13**.

The grammatical differences between American English and British English are far less obvious. They tend to be localised in very specific areas of grammar. Some differences may be observed in the use of prepositions (▶see **2.8**). Americans say *ten after twelve*, while Britons say *ten past twelve*. Americans say *in back of the house*, Britons say *behind the house*. In the choice of verb forms, too, we can see some systematic differences. American English tends to prefer the regular form of a verb when a choice is available, for example, *burned* in favour of *burnt*, *learned* in favour of *learnt* (▶see **2.3.8**).

Despite their differences, American English and British English, as well as all the other national varieties – Australian, Canadian, New Zealand, Indian, and so on – share a very extensive common core of vocabulary, spelling and grammar. It is this common core that makes them mutually intelligible. In this book, we are concerned with the core grammatical features of English, and especially with the core features of the two major varieties, American English and British English.

Grammatical variation across national varieties of English is currently the subject of a major research project, the International Corpus of English (ICE), which is being coordinated by the Survey of English Usage, University College London. For more information, see http://www.ucl.ac.uk/english-usage/.

Many of the citations in this grammar are taken from the British component of ICE (ICE-GB), and from parts of the American component (ICE-USA). In some cases, the originals have been shortened for illustrative purposes. Omissions are indicated by [. . .].

The grammatical hierarchy

The building blocks of grammar are sentences, clauses, phrases and words. These four units constitute what is called the grammatical hierarchy. We can represent the hierarchy schematically as shown overleaf.

SENTENCES

– consist of one or more:

CLAUSES

– consist of one or more:

PHRASES

– consist of one or more:

WORDS

In Chapter 1, we look at sentences in terms of their sentence 'elements' – subject, verb, object, etc. In Chapter 2 we turn our attention to the lower end of the hierarchy, and consider how words are classified into word classes. The following two chapters look at phrases and clauses respectively.

Sentences are at the top of the grammatical hierarchy, so they are often the largest units to be considered in a grammar book. However, in this book we also look briefly at some of the devices that are available for joining sentences to other sentences, and for organising them in continuous discourse. These topics are discussed later in the book ▶see **4.11**.

Words are at the bottom of the hierarchy, and for that reason some grammar books treat them as the smallest units in a language. However, the internal structure of a word can often play an important role. For instance, when we add the inflection *-er* to the adjective *old*, we create the comparative adjective *older*. In Chapter 5, we look at the internal structure of words, and especially at prefixes and suffixes. We also look at some of the methods that are available for creating new words, including 'blending' – combining parts of words, such as '*cam*' (from *camera*) and '*corder*' (from *recorder*), to create the new word *camcorder*. Chapter 5 concludes by looking at English spelling. It offers general rules for spelling, and discusses some common spelling problems – words like *affect* and *effect* which are easily and regularly confused with each other in writing.

Chapter 1

The elements of a simple sentence

1.1   Simple, compound, and complex sentences

In writing, a sentence is any sequence of words which begins with a capital letter and ends with a full stop (period), a question mark or an exclamation mark:

Paul plays football.

Amy prefers tennis.

Who lives in the house next door?

Where did you buy your car?

What a silly thing to say!

How big you've grown!

These are all **simple sentences.** We can combine two simple sentences using *but* or *and*:

[1]   Paul plays football.

[2]   Amy prefers tennis.

[1]+[2] Paul plays football *but/and* Amy prefers tennis.

A combination of two or more simple sentences is called a **compound sentence.**

A **complex sentence** contains another 'sentence-like' construction within it:

> When the plane landed, the ground crew removed the cargo.

Here, the sentence as a whole contains the sentence-like construction *When the plane landed*. We refer to this construction as a **clause**:

Sentence

⟵——————————————————⟶

Clause

⟵————⟶

When the plane landed   *the ground crew removed the cargo.*

We will discuss clauses, as well as complex sentences, in Chapter 4.

In this chapter we concentrate on simple sentences. A simple sentence is a sentence which contains no clause within it.

1.2   Subject and predicate

Typically, a simple sentence consists of a **subject** and a **predicate**. The subject is usually the first element in the sentence, while the rest of the sentence, including the **verb**, is the predicate. Here are some examples of subjects and predicates:

Subject	Predicate
Amy	laughed.
Paul	plays football.
The house	is very old.
The detectives	interviewed the suspects.

The predicate always contains at least a verb. In these examples, the verbs are *laughed*, *plays*, *is* and *interviewed*.

1.3 Identifying the subject

The subject (S) of a sentence can often be identified by asking a question beginning with *who* or *what*:

Amy laughed.

Q. *Who* laughed?

A. *Amy* (= S)

The house is very old.

Q: *What* is very old?

A: *The house* (= S)

In addition, the subject of a sentence has the following grammatical properties:

1   **Subject–verb inversion.** In a declarative sentence (a statement – ▶see **1.14.1**), the subject comes before the verb:

   Declarative: James (S) is (V) at school.

   When we change this to an interrogative sentence (a question – ▶see **1.14.2**), the subject and the verb change places with each other:

   Interrogative: Is (V) James (S) at school?

2   **Subject–verb agreement.** The subject of a sentence agrees in number (singular or plural) with the verb which follows it. Compare:

   Singular subject: *The dog barks* all night.

   Plural subject: *The dogs bark* all night.

Here, the form of the verb (*barks* or *bark*) is determined by whether the subject is singular (*the dog*) or plural (*the dogs*). This is known as subject–verb agreement.

However, subject–verb agreement only applies when the verb has a present-tense form. In the past tense, there is no agreement with the subject:

Singular subject: *The dog barked* all night.

Plural subject: *The dogs barked* all night.

Furthermore, agreement applies only to third-person subjects. For instance, the same verb form is used whether the subject is *I* (the first-person singular) or *we* (the first-person plural):

Singular subject: *I sleep* all night.

Plural subject: *We sleep* all night.

1.4   Verb types

The pattern of a simple sentence is largely determined by the type of verb it contains. There are three verb types: intransitive (▶see 1.4.1), linking (▶see 1.4.2) and transitive (▶see 1.4.3).

1.4.1 | *Intransitive verbs*

An **intransitive verb** can occur alone in the predicate of a sentence, because it requires no other sentence element to complete its meaning:

Amy *laughed.*

The baby *cried.*

The temperature *dropped.*

The sky *darkened.*

The ship *disappeared.*

Each of these sentences contains just a subject and a verb, so their pattern is:

Sentence pattern 1

―――――――――――――

S   V

Amy   laughed.

1.4.2 Linking verbs

Unlike other verbs (such as *destroy, sing, laugh, eat, break*), the verb *be* does not denote any kind of 'action'. Instead, it links the subject to another element following the verb:

Paul *is* 12.

Here, we would not say that Paul performs any 'action' in 'being 12'. The verb simply links the two elements *Paul* and *12*, and for this reason, we call it a **linking verb**.

Be is by far the most common linking verb, though there are several others:

David *seems* unhappy.

The house *appeared* empty.

She *looks* uncomfortable.

The animals *became* restless.

The crowd *went* wild.

The element following a linking verb is called the **subject complement** (SC – ▶see 1.5). Therefore the pattern in these sentences is:

Sentence pattern 2		
S	V	SC
Paul	is	12.

1.4.3 | Transitive verbs

A **transitive verb** is a verb which cannot stand alone in the predicate of a sentence. Instead, it requires another sentence element to complete its meaning. Consider, for example, the verb *destroy*. This verb needs an element following it – one cannot simply *destroy*, one has to destroy *something*. Compare:

*The soldiers *destroyed*.

The soldiers *destroyed the village*.

Destroy, therefore, is a transitive verb. Further examples of transitive verbs include:

The generator *produces* electricity.

Jim *bought* a new house.

She really *enjoyed* her party.

Christopher Wren *designed* St Paul's Cathedral.

In these examples, the element that completes the meaning of the transitive verb (*the village, electricity, a new house*, etc.), is called the **direct object** (DO – ▶see 1.6). These sentences therefore display the pattern:

Sentence pattern 3

S   V   DO

The soldiers   destroyed   the village.

Many verbs have both intransitive (▶see 1.4.1) and transitive uses, sometimes with different meanings. Compare the following pairs:

Intransitive: *The boys grew* (S+V)

Transitive: *The boys grew mushrooms* (S+V+DO)

Intransitive: *The old man shook* (S+V)

Transitive: *The old man shook his fist* (S+V+DO)

Intransitive: *Simon sings* (S+V)

Transitive: *Simon sings ballads* (S+V+DO)

1.5   Subject complement

When the verb in a sentence is a linking verb, such as *be*, *seem*, *appear*
(▶see 1.4.2), the element following the verb is called the subject complement (SC):

Paul is *12*.

The subject complement typically denotes an attribute or property of the
subject. In this example, it denotes the age of the subject, *Paul*. Here are
some more examples of subject complements:

	Subject complement
My tea is	*cold.*
Mr Johnson is	*an engineer.*
The house appeared	*empty.*

1.6 Direct object

In the sentence *The soldiers destroyed the village*, we refer to the element *the village* as the direct object (DO). The DO is required to complete the meaning of the verb *destroyed*. Here are some more examples of sentences with DOs:

	Direct object
The detectives interviewed	*the suspects.*
This shop sells	*excellent bread.*
The storm caused	*a lot of damage.*

The DO is typically that part of a sentence which is affected by the 'action' of the verb. It can often be identified by asking a question beginning with *what* or *whom*:

The soldiers destroyed the village.

Q. *What* did the soldiers destroy?

A. *The village* (= DO)

The detectives interviewed the suspects.

Q. *Whom* did the detectives interview?

A. *The suspects* (= DO)

1.7   Indirect object

Some sentences contain two objects:

> We gave *David the prize.*

The two objects here are *David* and *the prize.* The element *the prize* is the direct object (**What did we give David?** – *The prize*). The other object, *David*, is called the **indirect object** (IO). Here are some more examples of sentences with two objects:

	Indirect object	Direct object
They awarded	James	a salary increase.
She told	her husband	the news.
I asked	him	a question.
The postman brought	us	a package.

When two objects are present in a sentence, the indirect object comes first, followed by the direct object, so the pattern is:

Sentence pattern 4			
S	V	IO	DO
We	gave	David	the prize.

Pattern 4 sentences can often be rewritten as follows:

> We gave David the prize.   ~²We gave the prize to David.

---

² The symbol ~ is used throughout this book to mean 'may legitimately be changed to'.

Object complement

An **object complement** (OC) describes an attribute of the direct object (▶see 1.6):

> The dye turned the water *blue*.

Here, *blue* is the object complement. It describes an attribute (the colour) of *the water*, which is the direct object. Here are some more examples:

> His comments made me *angry* (OC).

> They elected Amy *Treasurer* (OC).

> Mary called Simon *a fool* (OC).

Object complements occur after the object which they describe, so the pattern in these sentences is:

Sentence pattern 5			
S	V	DO	OC
The dye	turned	the water	blue.

At first glance, some Pattern 5 sentences may look very similar to Pattern 4 sentences. Compare:

> [1] **Pattern 5:** The Manager made Jones *captain*.
> (S+V+DO+OC)

> [2] **Pattern 4:** The Manager made Jones *coffee*.
> (S+V+IO+DO)

The grammatical difference between these two can be seen when we rephrase them. Sentence [2] can be rephrased as:

> [2a] The Manager made coffee *for Jones*.

In contrast, sentence [1] cannot be rephrased in the same way:

[1a]   *The Manager made captain *for Jones.*

The element *captain* in [1] describes an attribute of *Jones* (Jones is captain), so *captain* is an object complement.

Similarly, compare:

Pattern 5: Mary called Simon *a fool.* (Simon is a fool)

Pattern 4: Mary called Simon *a taxi.* (. . . called a taxi for Simon)

1.9   The five sentence patterns

In the previous sections, we looked at the following sentence elements:

Subject	S	(▶see 1.3)
Verb	V	(▶see 1.4)
Subject complement	SC	(▶see 1.5)
Direct object	DO	(▶see 1.6)
Indirect object	IO	(▶see 1.7)
Object complement	OC	(▶see 1.8)

These elements combine to form the five basic sentence patterns shown in Table 1.

Notice that the elements S (subject) and V (verb) are present in all the patterns. This means that all sentences contain at least a subject and a verb. There is one exception to this: imperative sentences like *Look!* and *Move over!* have a verb, but no subject (▶see 1.14.3).

Table I Sentence patterns and verb types

Sentence pattern	Verb type	Examples
I S+V	Intransitive	Amy (**S**) laughed (**V**). The audience (**S**) applauded (**V**). The temperature (**S**) dropped (**V**).
2 S+V+SC	Linking	My tea (**S**) is (**V**) cold (**SC**). My friend (**S**) is (**V**) ill (**SC**). David (**S**) seems (**V**) unhappy (**SC**).
3 S+V+DO	Transitive	The soldiers (**S**) destroyed (**V**) the village (**DO**). The police (**S**) interviewed (**V**) the suspects (**DO**). The storm (**S**) caused (**V**) a lot of damage (**DO**).
4 S+V+IO+DO	Transitive	We (**S**) gave (**V**) David (**IO**) the prize (**DO**). They (**S**) awarded (**V**) James (**IO**) a salary increase (**DO**). I (**S**) asked (**V**) him (**IO**) a question (**DO**).
5 S+V+DO+OC	Transitive	The dye (**S**) turned (**V**) the water (**DO**) blue (**OC**). His comments (**S**) made (**V**) me (**DO**) angry (**OC**). They (**S**) elected (**V**) Amy (**DO**) President (**OC**).

Key: S = subject; **V** = verb; **SC** = subject complement; **DO** = direct object; **IO** = indirect object; **OC** = object complement

1.10   Active and passive sentences

Sentences are either **active** or **passive**.

> **Active:**   Shakespeare *wrote* King Lear.
>
> **Passive:**   King Lear *was written* by Shakespeare.

The active sentence has the pattern S+V+DO (Pattern 3 – ►see Table 1). The direct object *King Lear* becomes the subject of the passive version, while *Shakespeare*, the subject of the active version, moves to the end of the passive version.

Passive sentences are formed by adding the passive auxiliary *be* (►see **2.7.3**) and by using a different form of the verb – in this case *written* instead of *wrote*. On the verb forms, ►see **2.3.1**.

Here are some more examples of active and passive pairs:

> **Active:**   The burglar broke a pane of glass.
>
> **Passive:**   A pane of glass was broken by the burglar.

> **Active:**   The curator shows the manuscript to visitors.
>
> **Passive:**   The manuscript is shown to visitors by the curator.

> **Active:**   The police are seeking witnesses.
>
> **Passive:**   Witnesses are sought by the police.

The 'by-phrase' (*by the burglar, by the curator, by the police*) is sometimes omitted, leaving an **agentless passive**:

> **Active:**   The burglar broke a pane of glass.
>
> **Passive:**   A pane of glass was broken by the burglar.
>
> **Agentless Passive:**   A pane of glass was broken.

Only sentences with a transitive verb (►see **1.4.3**) can have a passive version. However, a small number of verbs cannot be passivized, even though they are transitive in the active version. These include *have*, *resemble*, and *suit*:

Active: James *has* a new car.

Passive: **A new car *is had* by James.

Active: Paul *resembles* Anthony.

Passive: **Anthony *is resembled* by Paul.

Active: That colour *suits* you.

Passive: **You *are suited* by that colour.

The distinction between an active sentence and a passive sentence is called
voice.

1.11   Adjuncts

The five sentence patterns (Table 1, p. 20) can all be extended by the
use of **adjuncts**. Adjuncts (A) contribute optional, additional information
to a sentence. For example, the S+V sentence *The sky darkened* can be
extended by the addition of adjuncts, to become:

The sky darkened *suddenly*. (S+V+A)

The sky darkened *before the hailstorm*. (S+V+A)

The sky darkened *at about 9 o'clock*. (S+V+A)

In the following examples, we show how each of the five sentence patterns
may be extended by adding an adjunct:

Pattern 1: S+V+A

Amy laughed *loudly* (A).

Pattern 2: S+V+SC+A

My tea is cold *as usual* (A).

Pattern 3: S+V+DO+A

The soldiers destroyed the village *deliberately* (A).

Pattern 4: S+V+IO+DO+A

We gave David the prize *in the end* (A).

Pattern 5: S+V+DO+OC+A

The dye turned the water blue *in just a few seconds* (A).

Adjuncts can also appear at the beginning of a sentence, before the subject:

Suddenly, the sky darkened. (A+S+V)

Before the hailstorm, the sky darkened. (A+S+V)

At about 9 o'clock, the sky darkened. (A+S+V)

And finally, adjuncts can co-occur. That is, more than one adjunct can occur in the same sentence:

Before the hailstorm (A) the sky darkened *suddenly* (A).

Unfortunately (A) my tea is cold *as usual* (A).

On Sunday (A), *after the game* (A), we met Simon *outside the stadium* (A).

In contrast with this, a simple sentence can contain just one subject, one verb, one direct object, and so on.

1.12 The meanings of adjuncts

Adjuncts (▶see 1.11) contribute various types of additional information to a sentence. The principal information types are set out below.

1 **Time** (*when* something happens):

The play opened *yesterday*.

Our guests arrived *at seven o'clock*.

We visit Greece *every year*.

2 **Place** (*where* something happens):

> Amy attended university *in New York*.

> We met Simon *outside the restaurant*.

> I saw David *at the swimming pool*.

3 **Manner** (*how* something happens):

> She sings *beautifully*.

> The children listened *intently*.

> *Gradually* the room filled with smoke.

▶See also **4.6**.

1.13 Vocatives

A vocative is used to identify the person or persons to whom a sentence is addressed:

> *James*, your dinner is ready.

> Come inside, *children*.

> *Doctor*, I need a new prescription.

> The car was parked behind the building, *your Honour*.

> I'm sorry I'm late, *everyone*.

> *Ladies and gentlemen*, thank you for that warm welcome.

Like adjuncts (▶see **1.11**), vocatives are optional elements in sentence structure.

1.14   Sentence types

There are four major sentence types: declarative (►see 1.14.1), interrogative (►see 1.14.2), imperative (►see 1.14.3), and exclamative (►see 1.14.4).

1.14.1 │ *Declarative sentences*

A **declarative sentence** is typically used to convey information or to make a statement:

This is Gladstone Park.

David is listening to music.

Simon bought a new house.

James retired in 1998.

In a declarative sentence, the subject usually comes first, and it is followed by the verb. Declarative sentences are by far the most common type. All the sentences we have looked at so far have been declarative sentences.

1.14.2 │ *Interrogative sentences*

An **interrogative sentence** is used in asking a question, and in seeking information:

Is this Gladstone Park?

Have you found a job yet?

Did you receive my e-mail?

Do you take sugar?

Specifically, these are called **yes–no interrogatives**, because they expect either *yes* or *no* as the response.

Alternative interrogatives offer two or more alternative responses:

> Do you want tea or coffee?

> Is that a Picasso or a Dali?

Wh-interrogatives are introduced by a word beginning with *wh*, and they expect an open-ended response:

> *What* happened?

> *Where* do you work?

> *Who* won the FA Cup in 1999?

The word *how* may also introduce an interrogative:

> *How* do you forward an e-mail?

> *How* can I get to Charing Cross?

> *How* is your mother?

1.14.3 | *Imperative sentences*

An **imperative sentence** is used to issue orders or instructions:

> Wait a minute.

> Take the overnight train from King's Cross.

> Release the handbrake.

> Cut the meat into cubes.

Imperative sentences usually have no subject, as in these examples. However, the subject *you* may sometimes be included for emphasis:

> Don't *you* believe it.

> *You* fix it (if you're so clever).

| 1.14.4 | *Exclamative sentences* |

Exclamative sentences are exclamations, and they are introduced by *what* or *how*:

> *What* a fool I've been!

> *What* a lovely garden you have!

> *How* true that is!

> *How* big you've grown!

In exclamative sentences, *what* is used to introduce noun phrases (▶<u>see</u> <u>**3.2**</u>), while *how* introduces all other types.

The four sentence types – declarative, interrogative, imperative and exclamative – have different grammatical forms. However, there is no one-to-one relationship between the form of a sentence and its role in communication. For instance, the following sentence has a declarative form:

> You need more money.

However, if this is spoken with a rising intonation, it becomes a question:

> You need more money?

Conversely, rhetorical questions have the form of an interrogative sentence, but they are really statements:

> Who knows? (= Nobody knows.)

1.15   Fragments and non-sentences

All the sentences we have looked at so far have been grammatically complete. Grammatically complete sentences typically contain at least a subject and a verb. However, a great deal of communication consists of incomplete sentences or **fragments**. In conversation, for instance, speakers often omit the subject, especially when the subject is *I*:

Must set my alarm clock tonight.

Caught the early train.

Can't see anything.

In these cases, the subject *I* is understood.

Fragments are also commonly used in response to questions:

Speaker A: What did you buy for Sandra?

Speaker B: *A gold necklace.*

Speaker B's utterance is a fragment, which we interpret in the same way as the complete sentence *I bought a gold necklace for Sandra.*

Newspaper headlines are often highly compressed, so that complete sentences are reduced to fragments:

GOVERNMENT IN PENSIONS SCANDAL

This fragment has no verb, but we interpret it as the complete sentence *The Government is involved in a pensions scandal.*

We refer to these as fragments because we can interpret them in the same way as grammatically complete sentences. Only some of the sentence elements are missing.

Non-sentences have no sentence structure at all, and they generally occur without any surrounding context. They are frequently used in public signs and notices:

Exit

No Parking

Motorway Ahead

Paddington, 2 miles

10% Off

Closing Down Sale

Ticket Office

Non-sentences in conversational English include *bye, goodbye, hello, no, ok, right, sure, thanks, thanks very much, yes,* as well as the interjections *ouch!, ow!, phew!, yippee!, yuk!*

Fragments and non-sentences are a major feature of informal spoken English. In fact, they account for about one-third of all utterances in conversation.

Chapter 2

Words and word classes

Open and closed word classes

Words may be divided into the following major word classes:

Word class	Examples
Nouns	*brother, child, China, ecology, James, tree*
Main verbs	*break, consider, destroy, eat, sing, talk*
Adjectives	*angry, cold, foolish, happy, tidy, young*
Adverbs	*carefully, gradually, happily, slowly*
Pronouns	*I, me, my, you, he, his, her, we, our*
Auxiliary verbs	*can, could, do, may, might, will, would*
Prepositions	*after, at, for, in, of, over, with, without*
Conjunctions	*although, and, because, but, or, when*
Articles	*a, an, the*
Numerals	*one, two, twenty, first, second, third*

Some word classes are **open**, that is, they admit new words as members as the need arises. The major open classes are the first two above – nouns and main verbs. The class of nouns is potentially infinite, since it is continually being expanded as new discoveries are made, new products are developed and new ideas are explored. In recent years, for example, developments in computer technology have given rise to many new nouns, including:

2.1

Open and closed word classes

bitmap	modem
CD-ROM	multimedia
dotcom	newsgroup
e-commerce	pixel
e-mail	voicemail
Internet	website
laptop	

These developments have also given rise to some new verbs:

download	right-click
upload	double-click
reboot	

The adjective and adverb classes also admit new members from time to time, though far less prolifically than the class of nouns. The class of numerals is open, since we can always add 1 to a number to make a new number.

In contrast with this, prepositions, for instance, belong to a **closed** word class. We never invent new prepositions (words like *after*, *at*, *before*, *in*, *with*) simply because we never need them.

2.2 Nouns

Nouns denote both concrete objects and abstract entities:

Concrete	Abstract
book	anger
chair	difficulty
dog	eagerness
grass	history
lake	information
house	progress
tree	terror

Many nouns can be identified by their characteristic endings:

-ence	*absence, difference, evidence, experience*
-ment	*embarrassment, experiment, government, treatment*
-tion	*education, information, situation, vegetation*
-ism	*defeatism, optimism, populism, symbolism*

For more examples of noun endings, ▶<u>see **5.3**</u>.

2.2.1 | *Singular and plural nouns*

Most nouns have two forms, a **singular** form and a **plural** form. Regular nouns form the plural by adding *-s* to the singular:

Singular	Plural
boy	boys
table	tables

However, some very frequent nouns have irregular plurals:

Singular	Plural
man	men
woman	women
child	children
foot	feet
goose	geese
mouse	mice
tooth	teeth
sheep	sheep

The distinction between singular and plural is called **number contrast**.

For more on the spelling of plural nouns, ▶see **5.11**.

| 2.2.2 | *Common and proper nouns* |

Proper nouns are the names of individual people and places, including geographical features such as roads, rivers, mountains and oceans:

Patrick	Hong Kong
Nelson Mandela	Euston Road
China	Atlantic Ocean
Paris	River Thames
New Delhi	Mount Everest

The names of institutions, newspapers, buildings and ships are also proper nouns:

The Wall Street Journal	London Underground
The Royal Albert Hall	Titanic
Harvard University	Mayflower
Millennium Dome	

Finally, proper nouns include the days of the week, the months of the year and other periods of the calendar:

Monday	Christmas
Tuesday	Passover
January	Ramadan
February	Thanksgiving

Proper nouns are written with an initial capital (upper-case) letter. All other nouns are **common** nouns. Since proper nouns usually refer to unique individuals, places, or events in the calendar, they do not normally have a plural form. However, they may take a plural ending when number is specifically being referred to:

There are two *Patricks* in my class.

2.2.3 | *Countable and uncountable nouns*

Singular nouns denote just one instance, while plural nouns denote more than one instance:

Singular	Plural
one *boy*	two *boys*, three *boys*, four *boys* ...
one *day*	two *days*, three *days*, four *days* ...
one *computer*	two *computers*, three *computers*, four *computers* ...

These nouns are called **countable nouns**. In contrast, some nouns cannot be counted in this way:

*one *advice*, two *advices*, three *advices* ...

*one *furniture*, two *furnitures*, three *furnitures* ...

*one *software*, two *softwares*, three softwares ...

These nouns are called **uncountable nouns**. Uncountable nouns refer to things which are considered as indivisible wholes, and therefore cannot be counted.

Uncountable nouns have two important grammatical features:

1   They have a singular form (*advice, furniture, software*), but no plural form (**advices*, **furnitures*, **softwares*)

2   They do not take *a* or *an* before them (**an advice*, **a furniture*, **a software*)

Other uncountable nouns include: *fun, information, health, honesty, luck, luggage, mud, music, traffic.*

2.2.4 Genitive nouns

Genitive nouns denote possession:

> *John's* car = the car belonging to John

> the *baby's* toys = the toys belonging to the baby

The **genitive** (sometimes called genitive case) is formed:

1   By adding *'s* (apostrophe *s*) to a singular noun:

the *baby*	the *baby's* toys
our *son*	our *son's* wife
the *President*	the *President's* office

2   If the noun already has an *-s* ending because it is plural, we add the apostrophe alone to form the genitive:

the *Farmers*	the *Farmers'* Union
two *doctors*	two *doctors'* reports

3   With irregular plural nouns (▶**see 2.2.1**), the genitive is formed by adding apostrophe *s*, just as in (1) above:

the *children*	the *children's* clothes
the *men*	the *men's* toiletries
the *women*	the *women's* group
the *people*	the *people's* decision

4   Nouns ending in *-s*, in which the *-s* does not denote a plural, generally take an apostrophe alone:

Prince *Charles*	Prince *Charles'* children
Martin *Nichols*	Martin *Nichols'* house

However, apostrophe *s* is also sometimes added:

> Prince *Charles's* children.

2.2.5 | *Dependent and independent genitives*

Genitives are either dependent or independent. A **dependent** genitive is followed by a noun:

the *child's* toys

a *student's* essay

Caroline's friend

An **independent** genitive is not followed by a noun:

a friend of *Caroline's*

a colleague of *Frank's*

an old army pal of *Jim's*

An independent genitive is often used in referring to relationships between people, as in these examples. Notice that this construction has a very specific meaning. The independent genitive *a friend of Caroline's* does not mean the same as the dependent genitive *Caroline's friend*:

Independent: We met a friend of Caroline's in Spain.

Dependent: We met Caroline's friend in Spain.

The independent genitive means 'one of Caroline's friends', who may or may not be known to the hearer. In contrast, the dependent genitive means 'one specific friend', who is assumed to be known to the hearer.

Independent genitives are also used in references to places and businesses:

She stayed at *Rebecca's*   = Rebecca's house

I ran into Jim in *Sainsbury's*   = Sainsbury's supermarket

I left my wallet in the *barber's*   = the barber's shop

▶See also **Possessive pronouns**, **2.6.2**.

2.2.6 | The gender of nouns

The gender of nouns plays an important role in the grammar of some languages. In French, for instance, a masculine noun such as *ciel* (sky) requires the masculine form (*le*) of the definite article (*le ciel* = the sky). A feminine noun, such as *mer* (sea) requires the feminine form (*la*) of the definite article (*la mer* = the sea).

In English, however, nouns are not in themselves either masculine or feminine. They do not have grammatical gender, though they may refer to male or female people or animals:

The *waiter* was very efficient.   The *waitress* was very efficient.

The *tiger* roars at night.   The *tigress* roars at night.

These spelling differences (*waiter/waitress, tiger/tigress*) reflect distinctions of sex, but they have no grammatical implications. We use the same definite article *the* whether we are referring to *the waiter* or *the waitress*, *the tiger* or *the tigress*.

Similarly, the natural distinctions reflected in such pairs as *brother/sister*, *father/mother*, and *king/queen* have no implications for grammar. While they refer to specific sexes, these words are not masculine or feminine in themselves.

However, gender is important in English when we replace a noun with a **pronoun** (▶see **2.6**):

The *waiter* was very efficient.   ~*He* was very efficient.

The *waitress* was very efficient.   ~*She* was very efficient.

Here, the choice of pronoun (*he* or *she*) is determined by the sex of the person being referred to. Gender differences are also seen in other pronoun pairs, including *his/her* and *himself/herself*.

▶See also **Gender-neutral pronouns**, **2.6.4**.

2.3   Main verbs

Main verbs include:

believe	read
break	see
destroy	run
eat	sleep
go	teach
love	walk
meet	work

We distinguish them here from the **auxiliary verbs** (▶see **2.7**) such as *can, could, may, might, must, shall, should, will, would*. Main verbs can occur as the *only* verb in a sentence:

Caroline *eats* pizza.

In contrast, an auxiliary verb such as *will* cannot occur alone:

*Caroline *will* pizza.

Instead, an auxiliary verb always occurs with a main verb:

Caroline *will eat* pizza.

2.3.1   *The five verb forms*

Verbs have five forms:

1	the base form	Amy decided to *walk* to school.
2	the *-s* form	Amy *walks* to school.
3	the past form	Amy *walked* to school.
4	the *-ed* form	Amy has *walked* to school.
5	the *-ing* form	Amy is *walking* to school.

The endings -s, -ed, and -ing are called **inflections** (▶see **5.8**). The inflections are added to the **base form** of the verb.

In regular verbs, two of the forms are identical: the past form (*walked*)
and the -ed form (*walked*). However, we must distinguish between these
two forms because they are not always identical. For example, the irregular verb *write* has the following five forms:

1	the base form	Amy loves to *write* poetry.
2	the -s form	Amy *writes* poetry.
3	the past form	Amy *wrote* a poem.
4	the -ed form	Amy has *written* a poem.
5	the -ing form	Amy is *writing* a poem.

See the Appendix for a list of irregular verbs, together with their five
forms.

In the following sections, we look at each of the five verb forms in turn.

2.3.2 | The base form

The base form of a verb is used:

1   After *to*:

> We decided to *walk*.

> Amy loves to *write* poetry.

The combination of *to* and the base form of a verb is called the
infinitive.

2   In the present tense, with all subjects except *he*, *she*, or *it* (the
third-person singular pronouns – ▶see **2.6.1**):

> I *walk*   we *walk*
>
> you *walk*   they *walk*

Compare:

> he/she/it *walks* (= the -s form – ►<u>see **2.3.3**</u>)

3 In imperative sentences (►<u>see **1.14.3**</u>):

> *Walk* quickly.

> Don't *move*.

> *Leave* your coat here.

4 In the subjunctive (►<u>see **3.3.6**</u>):

> I insist that she *resign* immediately.

2.3.3 | The -s form

The -s form of a verb is produced by adding -s to the base form. It is used only in the present tense, when the subject of the verb is *he*, *she*, or *it* (the third-person singular pronouns – ►<u>see **2.6.1**</u>):

> She *walks* to school.

> Amy *writes* poetry.

Compare:

> I *walk* to school. (= the base form, ►<u>see **2.3.2**</u>)

2.3.4 | The past form

The past form of a verb is produced by adding -ed to the base form. It is used for the past tense, with all subjects:

> I *cooked* dinner last night.

> You *cooked* dinner last night.

David *cooked* dinner last night.

We *cooked* dinner last night.

The children *cooked* dinner last night.

2.3.5 | The -ed form

Like the past form (▶see **2.3.4**), the -ed form of a verb is produced by adding -ed to the base form. The -ed form is used:

1   After the passive auxiliary *be* (▶see **2.7.3**):

The play was *directed* by Trevor Nunn.

The Queen was *shown* to her seat.

Our suitcases were *stolen* from the hotel.

Two new scenes were *written* for the final version.

2   After the perfective auxiliary *have* (▶see **2.7.5**):

Trevor Nunn has *directed* many plays.

The Mayor has *shown* the Queen to her seat.

Someone had *stolen* our suitcases.

The scriptwriter had *written* two new scenes.

3   In subordinate clauses (▶see **4.1**):

Published in 1998, the book became a best-seller.

The term '-ed form' is a just a cover term. Only regular verbs actually end in -ed in this form (e.g. *was destroyed*). Irregular verbs display a very wide variety of endings in the -ed form (e.g. *begun, written, brought, shown, stolen*). ▶ See **Appendix**.

2.3.6 | The -ing form

The *-ing* form of a verb is produced by adding *-ing* to the base form. The *-ing* form is used:

1   After the progressive auxiliary *be* (▶<u>see **2.7.4**</u>):

        She is *walking* to school.

        Alan was *sleeping* when I arrived.

2   In subordinate clauses (▶<u>see **4.1**</u>):

        Paul slammed the door, *bringing* the ceiling down.

2.3.7 | Irregular verbs

Many of the most common verbs in English are **irregular**. This means that their past form and their *-ed* form are not produced in the usual way (that is, by adding *-ed* to the base form). For instance, the verbs *bring*, *choose* and *think* are irregular:

Base	-s	Past	-ed	-ing
bring	brings	brought	brought	bringing
choose	chooses	chose	chosen	choosing
think	thinks	thought	thought	thinking

The irregular verbs display a great diversity of spelling in the past form and in the *-ed* form (▶<u>see **Appendix**</u>). However, we can distinguish the following major groups:

1   The base form ends in *d*, and the past form and the *-ed* form end in *t*:

Base	-s	Past	-ed	-ing
bend	bends	bent	bent	bending
build	builds	built	built	building
send	sends	sent	sent	sending
spend	spends	spent	spent	spending

2   The base form has *i*, the past form has *a*, and the *-ed* form has *u*:

Base	-s	Past	-ed	-ing
begin	begins	began	begun	beginning
drink	drinks	drank	drunk	drinking
sing	sings	sang	sung	singing
swim	swims	swam	swum	swimming

3   The base form has *ee* or *ea*, and the past form and the *-ed* form have *e*:

Base	-s	Past	-ed	-ing
bleed	bleeds	bled	bled	bleeding
feed	feeds	fed	fed	feeding
keep	keeps	kept	kept	keeping
leave	leaves	left	left	leaving

4   The base form is identical to the past form and the *-ed* form:

Base	-s	Past	-ed	-ing
cut	cuts	*cut*	cut	cutting
hit	hits	*hit*	hit	hitting
put	puts	*put*	put	putting
quit	quits	*quit*	quit	quitting

5   The past form and the *-ed* form are identical, and end in *ought* or *aught*:

Base	-s	Past	-ed	-ing
bring	brings	*brought*	*brought*	bringing
buy	buys	*bought*	*bought*	buying
catch	catches	*caught*	*caught*	catching
teach	teaches	*taught*	*taught*	teaching

2.3.8 | Regular and irregular variants

Some irregular verbs have regular variants, which may be used for both the past form and the *-ed* form. In the following examples, both the regular *dreamed* and the irregular *dreamt* are used as the past form:

Regular: She *dreamed* she was on a hill overlooking Alexandria.

Irregular: I can't remember what I *dreamt* last night.

Similarly, the two variants *learnt* and *learned* are used as the *-ed* form in these examples:

Regular: Saddam Hussein ought to have *learned* from his experience.

Irregular: Rajiv may have *learnt* a lesson from this episode.

The following verbs also have regular and irregular variants:

burn	burned / *burnt*	dive	dived / *dove*
knit	knitted / *knit*	lean	leaned / *leant*
leap	leaped / *leapt*	prove	proved / *proven*
smell	smelled / *smelt*	spell	spelled / *spelt*
spill	spilled / *spilt*	spoil	spoiled / *spoilt*

In general, American English tends to prefer the regular variants (e.g. *I dreamed last night* rather than *I dreamt last night*).

2.3.9	*The verb* **be**

The verb *be* is very irregular, and exhibits a total of eight different forms. These forms are shown here:

Base form	Present-tense forms	Past-tense forms	*-ed* form	*-ing* form
be	I *am*	I *was*	been	being
	you *are*	you *were*		
	he/she/it *is*	he/she/it *was*		
	we *are*	we *were*		
	you *are*	you *were*		
	they *are*	they *were*		

Many of these forms are contracted in informal use:

I	'm	= *am*
he/she/it	's	= *is*
you/we/they	're	= *are*

Some of the forms also have contracted negative counterparts:

he/she/it	*isn't*	= *is not*
he/she/it	*wasn't*	= *was not*
you/we/they	*aren't*	= *are not*
you/we/they	*weren't*	= *were not*

In British English, the form *aren't* is used as a contraction of *am not* in **tag questions** (▶see **4.7.3**):

I am right, *aren't I?*

2.3.10 | *Multi-word verbs*

Multi-word verbs are combinations of a verb and one or more other words. The combinations function like a single verb. We distinguish three types:

1 **Phrasal verbs** are combinations of a verb and an adverb (▶see **2.5**):

The music *faded away* as we left the station.

The engine *cut out* just before landing.

Weigh up all the factors before making a decision.

Jeremy has been *trying out* the car in the Alps.

2 **Prepositional verbs** are combinations of a verb and a preposition (▶see **2.8**):

I'll *look into* the matter immediately.

Amy doesn't *approve of* smoking.

The barrister *called for* a unanimous verdict.

Paul is *looking after* his sister.

3   **Phrasal-prepositional verbs** are combinations of a verb, an adverb and a preposition:

I won't *put up with* this noise any longer.

I *went along with* their ideas for the sake of peace.

Members of the Huntu tribe *shy away from* violence.

Don't *give in to* his demands.

2.4   Adjectives

Adjectives express a quality or attribute of a noun:

a *happy* child	a *surly* person	*toxic* waste
an *old* man	*defective* brakes	a *greedy* child
a *red* flag	a *dangerous* road	a *large* hotel

Typical adjective endings include:

-ble   *accessible, comfortable, possible, responsible, terrible*

-ive   *constructive, deceptive, defective, furtive, interactive*

-ous   *continuous, delicious, enormous, rigorous, serious*

-y   *funny, greedy, happy, rainy, tasty, weary*

Most adjectives can occur before a noun, or after a linking verb (►see **1.4.2**):

a *violent* storm	~the storm was *violent*
a *delicious* meal	~the meal is *delicious*

However, a small number of adjectives are restricted to just one position. The adjective *afraid*, for instance, can only appear after a linking verb:

the children were *afraid*   *~the *afraid* children

Conversely, the adjective *chief* can only occur before a noun:

the *chief* result   *~the result is *chief*

In a small number of fixed expressions, an adjective appears immediately after the noun:

the people *responsible*

the Princess *Royal*

the heir *apparent*

the roadway *proper*

Adjectives can modify a small number of pronouns (▶see 2.6). They always follow the pronoun:

something *terrible*

someone *new*

nobody *special*

nothing *unusual*

2.4.1 | *Gradable adjectives*

Most adjectives can take a modifying word, such as *fairly*, *very* or *extremely*, before them:

fairly *cold*   very *cold*   extremely *cold*

The modifying word locates the adjective on a relative scale of intensity. In this example, the scale is from *fairly cold* to *extremely cold*. This characteristic of adjectives is called **gradability**.

The modifying words (*fairly, very, extremely*) are called **intensifiers** (▶see **2.5.3**).

| 2.4.2 | *Comparative and superlative adjectives* |

The adjective *cold* has two other forms, *colder* (the **comparative** form) and *coldest* (the **superlative** form). The form *cold* is called the **base** form. Most adjectives have these three forms. Here are some more examples:

Base form	Comparative form	Superlative form
new	newer	newest
old	older	oldest
dark	darker	darkest
big	bigger	biggest

The comparative form is produced by adding an *-er* ending to the base form. The superlative form is produced by adding an *-est* ending, again to the base:

Base *cold*   + *-er*   = comparative *colder*

Base *cold*   + *-est*   = superlative *coldest*

Some adjectives form the comparative and superlative using *more* and *most* respectively:

Base form	Comparative form	Superlative form
recent	more recent	most recent
important	more important	most important

In general, adjectives with one syllable in the base form take the *-er* and *-est* endings, while longer words use *more* and *most*:

Base form	Comparative form	Superlative form
warm	warmer	warmest
hopeful	more hopeful	most hopeful
beautiful	more beautiful	most beautiful
complicated	more complicated	most complicated

The adjectives *good* and *bad* have irregular comparative and superlative forms:

Base form	Comparative form	Superlative form
good	better	best
bad	worse	worst

| 2.4.3 | *Participipial adjectives* |

Participipial adjectives have the endings *-ed* or *-ing* that we normally associate with verbs (▶see **2.3.1**):

a *complicated* process   an *amazing* achievement

a *crazed* expression   a *boring* book

a *disabled* person   a *confusing* account

an *embarrassed* smile   a *fascinating* photograph

an *experienced* driver   a *rewarding* experience

a *talented* singer   a *staggering* result

Most participial adjectives have a corresponding verb (*to complicate*, *to amaze*, etc), but some do not. For example, there is no verb *to **talent***, corresponding to *a **talented** singer*.

Like other adjectives, participial adjectives may be **gradable**:

a *very complicated* process

an *extremely rewarding* experience

They also have comparative and superlative forms:

complicated   more complicated   most complicated

rewarding   more rewarding   most rewarding

▶See also **Adjective phrases**, **3.4**.

2.5 Adverbs

Many adverbs are formed by adding -*ly* to an adjective (►see **2.4**):

Adjective	Adverb
certain	certainly
extreme	extremely
exact	exactly
mad	madly
quick	quickly
slow	slowly
soft	softly

However, by no means all adverbs end in -*ly*. In particular, many adverbs referring to time and place have no distinctive ending. These include:

afterwards	now
away	soon
back	there
here	today
inside	tomorrow
never	yesterday

Note also that some adjectives end in -*ly*, including *costly*, *deadly*, *friendly*, *kindly*, *lively*, *timely*.

The words *hard* and *fast* can be used as both adverbs and adjectives:

Adverb: John works *hard*.

Peter drives *fast*.

Adjective: John is used to *hard* work.

Peter drives a *fast* car.

Adverbs are most commonly used to modify:

1   A verb:

Amy speaks *softly*.

David works *quickly*.

Paul will arrive *soon*.

2   An adjective:

fairly slow

terribly warm

extremely rude

3   Another adverb:

fairly slowly

very closely

extremely badly

| 2.5.1 | *Gradable adverbs* |

Many adverbs are gradable, that is, they can take a modifying word such as *fairly* or *very* which locates the adverb on a scale of intensity:

fairly slowly   *very* slowly   *extremely* slowly

fairly suddenly   *very* suddenly   *extremely* suddenly

2.5.2 | *Comparative and superlative adverbs*

Some adverbs exhibit three forms, the base form, the comparative form (ending in *-er*) and the superlative form (ending in *-est*):

Base form	Comparative form	Superlative form
John works *hard*.	Mary works *harder*.	Paul work *hardest*.
John drives *fast*.	Mary drives *faster*.	Paul drives *fastest*.

However, most adverbs express comparison using the words *more* and *most*:

Base form	Comparative form	Superlative form
importantly	more importantly	most importantly
probably	more probably	most probably
recently	more recently	most recently

2.5.3 | *Intensifiers*

An intensifier is a special type of adverb which is used to express intensity in an adjective or in another adverb. The most common intensifier is *very*:

very cold	*very* suddenly
very eager	*very* soon

Other intensifiers include *almost, completely, entirely, extremely, fairly, highly, quite, slightly, totally, utterly*.

In informal use, the word *pretty* is often used as an intensifier:

> The weather was *pretty* dreadful.

> You'll have to move *pretty* quickly.

2.5.4 The meanings of adverbs

Adverbs express three major types of meaning:

1   **Manner** adverbs indicate *how* something happens:

> Amy was playing *happily* in the garden.

> Paul writes *beautifully*.

> The thief crept *silently* along the roof.

> The passengers waited *calmly* for the lifeboats.

Other manner adverbs include *carefully, clearly, dangerously, heavily, heroically, patiently, quietly, quickly, rapidly, scientifically, slowly, softly, spontaneously.*

2   **Time** adverbs indicate *when* something happened, as well as frequency of occurrence:

> We visited Rome *recently*.

> Bernard has an interview *tomorrow*.

> I'm hoping to retire *soon*.

> *Sometimes* we go to Joe's in the High Street.

Other time adverbs include: *afterwards, again, always, never, now, often, presently, previously, rarely, then, today, yesterday.*

3   **Place** adverbs indicate a *place* or a *direction*:

> Leave your coat *there*.

> Why are you still *here*?

> She just turned and walked *away*.

> The car shot *forward* when I released the clutch.

Other place adverbs include: *backwards, downwards, everywhere, inside, outside, somewhere*.

▶See also **Adverb phrases**, **3.5**.

2.6   Pronouns

Many pronouns can be used as substitutes for nouns:

> *David* loves football. *He* supports Manchester United.

Here, the pronoun *he* substitutes for the noun *David*, to which it refers back. Using the pronoun means that we can avoid repeating the noun.

The major subclasses of pronouns are:

Personal pronouns: *I/me, he/him*, etc.   (▶see **2.6.1**)

Possessive pronouns: *my/mine, your/yours*, etc.(▶see **2.6.2**)

Reflexive pronouns: *myself, yourself*, etc.   (▶see **2.6.3**)

As Table 2 shows, these three subclasses are closely related to each other. We discuss each subclass in the following sections.

2.6.1 *Personal pronouns*

The **personal pronouns** (▶see Table 2, p. 58) exhibit contrasts for **person** (first person, second person, or third person), **number** (singular or plural),

Table 2
Personal, possessive, and reflexive pronouns

| Person | Number | Gender | Personal pronouns | | Possessive pronouns | | Reflexive pronouns |
			Subjective	Objective	Dependent	Independent	
1st	Singular	–	I	me	my	mine	myself
2nd	Singular	–	you	you	your	yours	yourself
3rd	Singular	Masculine	he	him	his	his	himself
		Feminine	she	her	her	hers	herself
		Non-personal	it	it	its	–	itself
1st	Plural	–	we	us	our	ours	ourselves
2nd	Plural	–	you	you	your	yours	yourselves
3rd	Plural	–	they	them	their	theirs	themselves

and **case** (subjective or objective). In addition, the third-person singular pronouns *he/she/it* exhibit a contrast for **gender** (masculine, feminine or non-personal).

The **subjective** forms of the personal pronouns are used when the pronoun is the subject of the sentence (▶see **1.2**):

I gave David a present.

You need a holiday, Sam.

He/she/it needs medical help.

We travelled by plane.

You should all complete an application form.

They enjoyed the film.

The **objective** forms are used in all other positions. These positions are:

1 After a verb (▶see **2.3**):

David gave *me* a present.

I'll see *you* soon.

The minister supports *him/her/it*.

Marie met *us* at the airport.

I'll bring *you* a nice surprise.

Susan telephoned *them*.

2 After a preposition (▶see **2.8**):

David gave it to *me*.

I'll probably get there before *you*.

She arrived after *him/her/it.*

He's not coming with *us.*

I'm tired talking to *you* people.

I'm writing a song for *them.*

There is no formal distinction between subjective *you* and objective *you*:

Subjective: *You* e-mailed me yesterday.

Objective: I e-mailed *you* yesterday.

Likewise, there is no formal distinction between singular *you* and plural *you*. When necessary, speakers and writers make the reference explicitly plural by expanding it, for instance by using *both of you, you both, all of you, you people, you children, you guys* (American English, informal).

2.6.2 | *Possessive pronouns*

The **possessive pronouns** (▶see Table 2, p. 58) exhibit contrasts for person (first person, second person, or third person) and for number (singular or plural). Like the personal pronouns (▶see 2.6.1), possessive pronouns have gender-based contrasts (masculine, feminine or non-personal) in the third-person singular.

Each possessive pronoun has two distinct forms, the dependent form and the independent form. **Dependent** possessives are used before a noun:

This is *my* car.

I've borrowed *your* computer.

She took *his/her/its* photograph.

We've lost *our* way.

They sold *their* house.

Independent possessives are used without a following noun. They most commonly occur after *of*, in independent genitives (▶<u>see **2.2.5**</u>):

a friend of *mine*

this partner of *yours*

a colleague of *his/hers*

an uncle of *ours*

that dog of *yours*

a relative of *theirs*

Independent possessives also occur in other positions, especially when the context makes clear what the pronoun refers to:

John's car is fast, but *mine* is cheaper to run.
('mine' = 'my car')

You are in my address book, but am I in *yours*?
('yours' = 'your address book')

The non-personal possessive pronoun *its* cannot be used independently. Compare:

The blue ribbon is *his*.

The red ribbon is *hers*.

*The yellow ribbon is *its*.

Its can only be used dependently, before a noun:

The horse shook *its* head.

2.6.3 | Reflexive pronouns

The **reflexive pronouns** end in *-self* (singular) or *-selves* (plural) (▶see Table 2, p. 58). They exhibit distinctions of person (first person, second person or third person), and number (singular or plural). The third-person singular reflexives (*himself/herself/itself*) show distinctions of gender (masculine, feminine or non-personal).

The reflexive pronouns are used to refer back to the subject of the same sentence:

> Michael was very badly injured and is now unable to feed *himself.*

Here, *himself* refers back to *Michael*, the subject of the sentence.

Less commonly, reflexive pronouns are used for emphasis:

> The Chancellor mentioned tax cuts, but he *himself* knows that the time is not right for reform.

Here, the reflexive *himself* co-occurs with the corresponding personal pronoun (subjective case) *he*. Similarly:

I myself	we ourselves
you yourself	they themselves
she herself	

2.6.4 | Gender-neutral pronouns

English lacks a gender-neutral pronoun in the singular. *He* is masculine, and *she* is feminine, but no pronoun exists to refer to people of unknown or unidentified sex (*it* can only be used to refer to objects and animals, not to people). Therefore a problem arises in sentences such as:

> Somebody has left *his* coat behind.

Clearly, the sex of 'somebody' is not known, so there is no way of knowing whether to use *his coat* or *her coat*. Traditionally, the masculine *his* has been used in these circumstances, as in the example above.

However, the arbitrary choice of *his* over *her* is now felt by many people to be unacceptably sexist.

A common solution is to use *his or her* (or *his/her*):

> Somebody has left *his or her* coat behind.

Likewise, the subjective pronouns *he or she*, *he/she* (and even *s/he*) are sometimes used as gender-neutral pronouns:

> Encourage your child to read when *he or she* reaches the age of 3.

However, this can be stylistically irritating, especially when it is repeated:

> *He or she* has to satisfy the jury that *he or she* is right.

> A candidate who wishes to enter the school before *his or her* eighteenth birthday may be asked to write to state *his or her* reasons.

Recently, the plural pronouns *their* (possessive) and *they* (subjective) are increasingly being used:

> Somebody has left *their* coat behind.

> Encourage your child to read when *they* reach the age of three.

2.6.5 | *Demonstrative pronouns*

The **demonstrative pronouns** are:

> this, that, these, those

This and *that* are singular, and are used with singular nouns:

> Do you need *this* pen?

> I really like *that* plant.

These and *those* are plural, and are used with plural nouns:

> Who owns *these* pens?

> We should buy some of *those* plants.

The demonstrative pronouns may also be used independently, that is, without a following noun:

> *This* is a great film.

> *That* is the challenge we face.

> *These* are very good apples.

> *Those* are quite cheap.

| 2.6.6 | *Relative pronouns* |

The **relative pronouns** are:

> who, whom, whose, which, that

Relative pronouns introduce a relative clause (▶see **4.3.2**):

> That's the man *who* lives beside us.

> That's the man *whom* we met yesterday.

> The problem *which* we're facing is very serious.

> The thing *that* worries me most is the overdraft.

Who and *whom* differ in case. *Who* is subjective:

> the man *who* lives beside us (cf. *the man* lives beside us)

Whom is objective:

> the man *whom* we met (cf. we met *the man*)

In formal contexts, and especially in writing, *whom* is used after a preposition (▶see **2.8**):

> the man on *whom* we rely
>
> the people with *whom* he used to work
>
> the person to *whom* it is addressed

In less formal contexts, including everyday speech, *whom* is often omitted altogether, and the preposition is moved to the end:

> the man we rely on
>
> the people he used to work with
>
> the person it is addressed to

2.6.7 | Pronoun it

The pronoun *it* has two major uses:

1   As a personal pronoun (▶see **2.6.1**) *it* can replace a third-person singular noun with non-human reference:

> *The car* skidded on ice.   ~*It* skidded on ice.
>
> Paul left *his coat* at school.   ~Paul left *it* at school.

2   *It* is used in expressions relating to the weather and to time:

> *It* is very cold.
>
> *It* rained last night.
>
> *It* is four o'clock.
>
> *It* is getting late.

This is sometimes called 'empty *it*' or 'dummy *it*', because *it* does not refer to anything in particular. Empty *it* is also used, with even vaguer reference, in many other expressions, including:

> Hold *it*! (= 'Stop')

> Take *it* easy!

> Can you make *it* to my party tonight?

▶See also **Cleft sentences** (**4.17**) and **Postponed subjects** (**4.18**).

| 2.6.8 | *Pronoun* one |

The pronoun *one* has two distinct uses:

1   Substitute *one* is used as a substitute for a noun that has been mentioned earlier:

> The black coat is nice but the green *one* is awful.

Here, the pronoun *one* substitutes for the noun *coat* (cf. *the green coat is awful*). Further examples of substitute *one* include:

> The problem is a complex *one*. (*one* = 'problem')

> The house was not a modern *one*, but it was comfortable.
> (*one* = 'house')

> I need a scanner so I'll just have to buy *one*.
> (*one* = 'a scanner')

Substitute *one* has a plural form, *ones*:

> The black coats are nice but the green *ones* are awful.

2   Generic *one* carries a generic meaning corresponding to 'people in general':

> *One* can't expect miracles.

One loses interest in everything when *one* has children.

Generic *one* has a genitive form *one's*:

When one is cold, *one's* capillaries close to minimise heat loss.

The corresponding reflexive pronoun (▶see **2.6.3**) is *oneself*:

One could easily find *oneself* out of a job.

Generic *one* is largely confined to written English. It can often be replaced by the less formal *you*:

You could easily find *yourself* out of a job.

2.7 Auxiliary verbs

In ▶**2.3** we introduced the distinction between a main verb such as *believe*, *eat*, *love*, and an auxiliary verb such as *can, may, might, will*. We said that a main verb can occur alone in a sentence:

Caroline *eats* pizza.

whereas an auxiliary verb such as *will* cannot occur alone:

*Caroline *will* pizza.

An auxiliary verb always occurs with a main verb:

Caroline *will eat* pizza.

Auxiliary verbs are sometimes called **helping verbs**, because they 'help' the main verb in some way. For instance, in *Caroline will eat pizza*, the auxiliary verb *will* expresses prediction.

Modal auxiliaries

The **modal auxiliary** verbs (or 'modals') are:

can	shall
could	should
may	will
might	would
must	

Here are examples of the modals in use:

We *can* visit the park if the weather's fine.

She *could* sense that something was wrong.

Susan *may* be late tomorrow morning.

I *might* see you again before I leave.

You *must* try a little harder.

I *shall* speak to him on his return.

David *should* join the army.

The play *will* open on 17 March.

I *would* love a game of tennis.

The modals have corresponding negative forms:

can	*can't/cannot*
could	*couldn't*
may	*mayn't* (British English – rare)
might	*mightn't*
must	*mustn't*

shall	*shan't* (British English – rare)
should	*shouldn't*
will	*won't*
would	*wouldn't*

Traditional grammars made a very sharp distinction between **shall** and **will**. They recommended that *shall* should be used to express future time with *I* as subject ('I *shall* arrive at six'), and that *will* should be used with all other subjects ('He *will* arrive at six.'). The reverse was recommended when expressing intention: 'I *will* work hard', but 'He *shall* work hard'.

In fact, these distinctions no longer apply in common use, if they ever did apply. The word *shall* has more or less disappeared from American English, and there is evidence that it is also in decline in British English, except perhaps in the most formal contexts. *Will* is the preferred form in both varieties.

2.7.2 | *The meanings of modal auxiliaries*

The modal auxiliary verbs express a very wide range of meanings. The principal meanings are:

Permission:	You *may* go in now.
	You *can* have a piece of chocolate.
Obligation:	You *must* complete both sides of the form.
Ability:	David *can* play the guitar.
	My grandfather *could* dance the Charleston.
Prediction:	I *will* be home at seven.
	We *shall* write as soon as possible.
Probability or Possibility:	This *may* be your last chance.
	You *must* be very tired.

| 2.7.3 | *The passive auxiliary* be |

The passive auxiliary *be* is used to form a passive sentence (▶see **1.10**):

> **Passive:**   The play *was* written by Tom Stoppard.

Compare:

> **Active:**   Tom Stoppard wrote the play.

The passive auxiliary is followed by the *-ed* form of a verb (▶see **2.3.5**).

The verb *get* is sometimes used as a passive auxiliary:

> It started to rain as I left the house, and I *got* soaked.

> At the end of the film, the villain *gets* shot by the police.

| 2.7.4 | *The progressive auxiliary* be |

As the name suggests, the **progressive auxiliary** *be* is used to denote action in progress:

> Paul *is* learning French.

It also has a past form:

> Paul *was* learning French.

A progressive auxiliary is followed by the *-ing* form of a verb (▶see **2.3.6**).

▶See also **Aspect**, **3.3.5**.

| 2.7.5 | *The perfective auxiliary* have |

The **perfective auxiliary** is *have*:

> Peter *has* injured his foot.

Caroline *has* finished her dissertation.

We *had* discussed the matter in 1996.

I *had* met Mr Callaghan before.

The perfective auxiliary is followed by the *-ed* form of a verb (▶<u>see</u> **2.3.5**).

▶<u>See also</u> **Aspect**, **3.3.5**.

2.7.6 | *Auxiliary* do

The auxiliary verb *do* has three main uses:

1   In forming questions:

>   *Do* you like Robert?
>
>   *Did* you enjoy the match?
>
>   *Does* your father use a computer?

2   In forming negative statements, with *not*:

>   I *do* not want it.
>
>   She *did* not graduate.
>
>   Simon *does* not eat cheese.

3   In negative imperatives, with *not*:

>   *Do* not touch that.
>
>   *Do* not move.

In informal use, *do not* is often contracted to *don't*:

>   *Don't* touch that.
>
>   *Don't* move.

2.7.7 | *Semi-auxiliaries*

Semi-auxiliaries are multi-word auxiliary verbs, including:

be about to	happen to	seem to
be going to	have to	tend to
be supposed to	mean to	used to

Like the other auxiliaries, semi-auxiliaries occur before a main verb:

The meeting *is about to* start.

David *is going to* retire at the end of August.

MPs *are supposed to* declare their financial interests.

Paul's car broke down so he *had to* walk.

Ottoman art *tends to* be very stylized.

2.8 Prepositions

The class of prepositions includes the following words:

about	below	in	to
across	between	into	toward(s)
after	by	of	under
against	down	off	until
at	during	on	up
before	for	over	with
behind	from	through	without

Prepositions are mainly used to introduce a noun phrase (▶see **3.2**):

after dark	*for* the children
across the road	*from* London

after the war	*under* suspicion
around the world	*with* mayonnaise
before my lunch	*without* fear

Multi-word prepositions are two- and three-word combinations which act as a unit:

according to	in accordance with
ahead of	in front of
apart from	in relation to
because of	in spite of
by means of	in terms of
due to	on behalf of

▶See also **Prepositional Phrases**, **3.6**.

2.9   Conjunctions

Conjunctions are used to link phrases and clauses together. There are two types:

1   **Coordinating conjunctions** (or simply 'coordinators') are used to link elements of *equal* grammatical status. The main coordinators are *and*, *but*, and *or*:

> The weather was [cold] *and* [wet].
>
> [Paul plays football] *and* [Amy enjoys tennis].
>
> [Simon is coming] *but* [he can't stay for long].
>
> [I read your book] *but* [I didn't enjoy it].
>
> Would you prefer [coffee] *or* [cappuccino]?
>
> [You can leave now] *or* [you can wait here].

The coordinator *or* is used with *either*:

You can have *either* [pizza] *or* [a hamburger].

In the negative counterpart of this, the coordinator *nor* is used with *neither*:

You can have *neither* [pizza] *nor* [a hamburger].

On **coordination**, ▶see **4.8**.

2   **Subordinating conjunctions** (or simply 'subordinators') introduce a subordinate clause:

Paul has to leave *because* he has a dental appointment.

Here, the main clause is *Paul has to leave*. The subordinate clause is *because he has a dental appointment*, and it is introduced by the subordinator *because*.

Other subordinators include:

although	that
after	unless
as	until
before	when(ever)
if	whereas
since	while

Multi-word subordinators include the following:

as long as	in order that
as soon as	provided that
as though	so long as
except that	such that

On **subordinate clauses**, ▶see **Chapter 4**.

2.10 **Articles**

The **articles** are *the* and *a/an*. Articles always occur before a noun, and they express the kind of reference that the noun has.

The **definite article** *the* is used to express definite reference:

> We saw *the* play in London.

This refers to 'a particular play', which must have been previously identified. Compare:

> We saw *a* play in London.

This refers to 'some unspecified play', which may be identified later:

> We saw *a* play in London. It was *The Chairs* by Ionesco.

The **indefinite article** is *a*, and its variant *an*. The choice between these variants is determined by the initial sound (not the spelling) of the word which follows the article. *A* is used when the following word begins with a consonant sound:

a chair	*a* large salary
a film	*a* UFO
a huge increase	

An is used when the following word begins with a vowel sound:

an active person	*an* MA course
an eager student	*an* overture
an examination	*an* x-ray
an L-plate	

The indefinite article is only used with singular, countable nouns. The definite article *the* is used with singular and plural nouns:

	Singular	Plural
Countable	*a castle*	**a castles*
	the castle	*the castles*
Uncountable	**a traffic*	–
	the traffic	–

Uncountable nouns have no plural form – ▶<u>see **2.2.3**</u>.

2.11   Numerals

Numerals include all numbers, whether written as words (*one*, *two*, *three*) or as digits (*1*, *2*, *3*). There are two main subclasses of numerals:

1   **Cardinal numerals** are used in counting. They refer to quantity:

> zero, nought, 0
>
> one, 1
>
> two, 2
>
> three, 3
>
> fifty, 50
>
> one hundred, 100
>
> one thousand, 1,000

2   **Ordinal numerals** refer to positions in a sequence:

> first, 1st
>
> second, 2nd
>
> third, 3rd
>
> fiftieth, 50th

one hundredth, 100th

one thousandth, 1,000th

By analogy with *first*, the word *last* is also an ordinal numeral, although it cannot be written as a digit.

Chapter 3

Phrases

3.1   The five phrase types

When we looked at pronouns (▶see **2.6**), we said that they are often used to replace a noun:

> David loves football. *He* supports Manchester United.

Here, the personal pronoun *he* replaces the noun *David*. But consider:

> The young boy who lives beside us loves football. *He* supports Manchester United.

In this case, *he* replaces the entire sequence *the young boy who lives beside us*. This is not a noun – it is a **noun phrase** (▶see **3.2**). We call it a noun phrase because its central word – *boy* – is a noun. More correctly, then, a pronoun can be used to replace a noun phrase.

There are five phrase types:

Phrase type	Examples
Noun phrase	*the young boy* Main word: noun *boy*
Verb phrase	*has been stolen* Main word: verb *stolen*
Adjective phrase	*very greedy* Main word: adjective *greedy*

Adverb phrase	*too quickly*
	Main word: adverb *quickly*
Prepositional phrase	*after the storm*
	Main word: preposition *after*

In a noun phrase, the main word is a noun, in a **verb phrase**, the main word is a verb and so on. Before looking at each of the five phrase types, a brief note on the word 'phrase'.

In grammar, a 'phrase' can consist of just one word, the main word alone. For instance, we say that both *greedy* and *very greedy* are adjective phrases. Why not simply say that *greedy* is an adjective? This is because the same rules apply to adjectives and adjective phrases. The same positional rules apply to *greedy* and to *very greedy*:

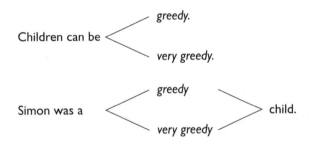

Instead of saying each time 'adjective or adjective phrase', it is simpler to say 'adjective phrase', and thereby include adjectives. So when we talk about phrases, remember that they may consist of just one word.

3.2   Noun phrases

Noun phrases have the following basic structure:

Determiner	Premodifier	Noun	Postmodifier
the	young	boy	who lives beside us

Determiners introduce noun phrases. Premodifiers and postmodifiers depend on the main word – the noun – and may be omitted.

3.2.1 | *Determiners*

The most common determiners are the articles (▶see **2.10**) – the definite article *the* and the indefinite article *a/an*.

> *the* tree

> *the* books

> *a* newspaper

> *an* optician

Other determiners include:

1   Possessive pronouns (▶see **2.6.2**):

> *my* books

> *your* ideas

> *his* diet

> *our* house

> *their* problem

2   Demonstrative pronouns (▶see **2.6.5**):

> *this* book

> *that* car

> *these* buildings

> *those* children

3   Numerals (►see **2.11**):

       one page

       two books

       second chance

       fourth paragraph

4   *Each, every, all, both* and *some*:

       each child

       every time

       all types

       some sugar

       both children

5   *Many, more* and *most*:

       many years

       more food

       most people

With certain restrictions, determiners can co-occur in a noun phrase:

    all the children

    our first home

    every second week

    his many talents

    all my many relatives

Determiners are unique to noun phrases. They do not occur in any of the other phrase types.

3.2.2 | *Premodifiers*

Premodifiers in a noun phrase occur before the noun, and after any determiners which may be present. In a noun phrase, the premodifier is typically an adjective:

> *green* eyes

> a *young* child

> some *beautiful* flowers

Premodifiers can co-occur, that is, more than one adjective can premodify the same noun:

> *lovely green* eyes

> an *innocent young* child

> some *beautiful yellow* flowers

As well as adjectives, the following words can function as premodifiers in a noun phrase:

1   Nouns (▶see **2.2**):

> *bank* manager   *bedroom* window

> *computer* manuals   the *Science* Museum

2   Genitive nouns (▶see **2.2.4**):

> *David's* homework   the *President's* office

> the *company's* accounts   our *child's* school

3.2.3 Postmodifiers

Postmodifiers in a noun phrase occur after the noun, and are most commonly prepositional phrases (▶see **3.6**) introduced by *of*:

a piece *of cheese*   the rotation *of the earth*

the top *of the hill*   a biography *of Mozart*

a view *of the sea*   the Museum *of Mankind*

The postmodifier may also be introduced by other prepositions:

the house *on the hill*

the Museum *in Kensington*

a coat *with a brown collar*

people *without computer skills*

As well as prepositional phrases, postmodifiers of noun phrases can be:

1   Relative clauses (▶see **4.3.2**):

the boy *who lives beside us*

the books *which you bought*

the film *that I enjoyed most*

2   *To*-clauses (▶see **4.2**):

a valve *to regulate the airflow*

a place *to store your clothes*

the first man *to walk on the moon*

Postmodifiers in a noun phrase can co-occur. The following examples illustrate noun phrases with two postmodifiers each:

a holiday [*for two*] [*in Rome*]

the shop [*in the High Street*] [*that sells fish*]

the photograph [*you took*] [*of Napoleon's tomb*]

3.2.4 | *Restrictive and non-restrictive postmodifiers*

A postmodifier in a noun phrase may be restrictive or non-restrictive. A **restrictive** postmodifer serves to define the noun:

The student *who got the highest grade* was given a prize.

Here, the postmodifier, *who got the highest grade,* is used to define exactly which student was given a prize. The postmodifier is therefore strictly necessary to the meaning of the sentence. Compare this with:

The student, *who comes from Birmingham,* was given a prize.

Here, the postmodifier, *who comes from Birmingham*, does not define exactly which student, from among all the students in the class, was given a prize. It simply conveys additional, optional information. This is a **non-restrictive** postmodifier.

In writing, non-restrictive postmodifiers are usually marked off with commas, as in the example above. In speech, the intonation pattern usually indicates their status.

3.2.5 | *Postmodifiers and complements*

Complements are a type of noun-phrase postmodifier (▶see **3.2.3**), but they have a much closer link with the noun than ordinary postmodifiers. Compare the following:

[I] Postmodifier:
The news *that he gave us today* was welcomed by everyone.

[2]   Complement:
> The news *that he intends to resign* was welcomed by everyone.

In [1], the postmodifier *that he gave us today* does not define the news. It does not tell us what the news was. In contrast with this, the complement in [2], *that he intends to resign*, plays a defining role. It tells us precisely what the news was (he intends to resign).

The distinction between a postmodifier and a complement is not just one of meaning. There is also a grammatical difference. In the postmodifier, we can usually replace *that* with *which*:

[1a] Postmodifier:
> The news *which he gave us today* was welcomed by everyone.

We cannot replace *that* with *which* in the complement:

[2a] Complement:
> *The news *which he intends to resign* was welcomed by everyone.

In general, nouns which take complements tend to have abstract reference. Here are some more examples:

> the realisation *that it wouldn't work*

> the fact *that no one came*

> the idea *that secularisation means something*

> the theory *that light is a wave motion*

3.2.6 *Apposition*

Apposition is a relationship between two noun phrases which have identical reference:

> the poet, Andrew Motion

The two noun phrases, *the poet* and *Andrew Motion,* refer to the same person, and are said to be in **apposition** to each other. Further examples of apposition include:

> the Yugoslav capital, Belgrade
>
> John's favourite food, pasta
>
> the SAC's chairman, Sir Alan Peacock
>
> our good friends, the Browns

Apposition is often used as a device for clarifying the meaning of the first noun phrase:

> the SB (the Polish secret police)
>
> the larynx (voice box)
>
> 230 litres (50 gallons)

In this type of 'clarifying' apposition, the word *or* is sometimes introduced between the two noun phrases:

> phototaxis, *or* light-directed motion
>
> vexillology, *or* the study of flags

▶See also **Pseudo-coordination**, **4.10**.

3.2.7 *The functions of noun phrases*

Noun phrases are grammatically very versatile. They can perform a wide range of functions in sentence structure (▶see **Chapter 1**). We illustrate the main functions of noun phrases here:

1   Subject (▶see **1.2**):

> *A large tile* fell from the roof.
>
> *Four people* entered the room.
>
> *The man who lives beside us* is unwell.

2   Subject complement (▶see 1.5):

Paul is *my nephew.*

She is *a teacher of English.*

That is *the wrong way to wire a plug.*

3   Direct object (▶see 1.6):

The plane left *the runway.*

I bought *a jar of coffee.*

Our teacher writes *detective stories.*

4   Indirect object (▶see 1.7):

She told *the chairman* the bad news.

I offered *the girl beside me* a drink.

It gives *people with disabilities* more independence.

5   Object complement (▶see 1.8):

He called her *an idiot.*

They appointed him *President of the Board of Trade.*

The unions made Britain *the country it is today.*

6   Adjunct (▶see 1.11):

Last week, our freezer broke down.

She's going to Harvard *next year.*

One day you'll regret quitting college.

3.3 **Verb phrases**

A verb phrase consists of a main verb (▶see **2.3**), which may be preceded by one or more auxiliary verbs (▶see **2.7**):

Auxiliary 1	Auxiliary 2	Auxiliary 3	Main Verb
may	have	been	*stolen*

3.3.1 | *The ordering of auxiliary verbs*

When two or more auxiliary verbs occur in a verb phrase, they observe the following relative order:

Modal – Perfective – Progressive – Passive

However, it is very unusual to find all four of the auxiliary verb types in the same verb phrase. Usually, a maximum of two or three auxiliaries will co-occur, as in the following examples:

Modal – Passive:
The seat *can be* lowered.

Progressive – Passive:
This lecture *is being* recorded.

Perfective – Progressive:
She *has been* collecting books for years.

Perfective – Passive:
The deficit *has been* reduced.

Modal – Perfective – Passive:
The concert *should have been* cancelled.

3.3.2 | Tense

There are two tenses in English, the present tense and the past tense. In regular verbs, the **present tense** is indicated by the *-s* form of the verb, when the subject is third-person singular:

3rd-person singular: he *walks*

she *walks*

it/David/the man *walks*

For all other subjects, the base form of the verb is used:

1st-person singular: I *walk*

2nd-person singular: you *walk*

1st-person plural: we *walk*

2nd-person plural: you *walk*

3rd-person plural: they *walk*

On the verb forms, ▶see **2.3.1**.

The **past tense** is indicated by an *-ed* verb ending, regardless of the subject:

1st-person singular: I *walked*

2nd-person singular: you *walked*

3rd-person singular: he/she/it/David/the man *walked*

1st-person plural: we *walked*

2nd-person plural: you *walked*

3rd-person plural: they *walked*

In these examples, only a main verb is present, so this verb carries the tense marker. When an auxiliary verb is present, the tense is indicated by the first (or only) auxiliary verb, and not by the main verb:

Present tense: The chairman *is* speaking.

Past tense: The chairman *was* speaking.

Present tense: The ambassador *has* done his duty.

Past tense: The ambassador *had* done his duty.

Present tense: A new script *is* being written.

Past tense: A new script *was* being written.

▶See also **Finite and non-finite verb phrases**, **3.3.4**.

| **3.3.3** | *Expressing future time* |

As we saw in ▶**3.3.2**, English has two tenses, the present tense and the past tense. The *-s* ending indicates present tense and the *-ed* ending indicates past tense. However, there is no ending to indicate the future, so it would be incorrect to speak of a 'future tense' in English. In fact, future time is very often expressed by using the present tense form of a verb:

Peter *arrives* next Friday.

Your flight *leaves* in ten minutes.

David *graduates* in September.

There are several other ways to express future time in English:

1   Modal auxiliary *will* (▶see **2.7.1**):

Peter *will* arrive next Friday.

Your flight *will* leave in ten minutes.

David *will* graduate in September.

The contracted form *'ll* is often used informally:

I*'ll* see you later.

2   Semi-auxiliary *be going to* (present tense) (▶<u>see **2.7.7**</u>):

Peter *is going to* arrive next Friday.

Your flight *is going to* leave in ten minutes.

David *is going to* graduate in September.

3   Progressive auxiliary *be* (present tense) + *-ing* verb (▶<u>see **2.7.4**</u>):

Peter *is arriving* next Friday.

Your flight *is leaving* in ten minutes.

David *is graduating* in September.

3.3.4 | *Finite and non-finite verb phrases*

Verb phrases are either finite or non-finite. A verb phrase is **finite** if the first (or only) verb exhibits tense (past or present). The following examples illustrate finite verb phrases. The finite ('tensed') verbs are in italics.

Simon *leaves* work at five.

Simon *left* early yesterday.

Simon *has* left.

Simon *had* left when I arrived.

Simon *has* been leaving early every day.

Notice that when two or more verbs occur in a finite verb phrase (e.g. *has left*, *has been leaving*), only the first verb indicates the tense. All the other verbs have **non-finite** forms. The non-finite verb forms are:

1 The base form, often introduced by *to* (*to leave*)
2 The *-ed* form (*left*)
3 The *-ing* form (*leaving*)

If the first (or only) verb in a verb phrase has one of these forms, then the verb phrase is non-finite:

> To *leave* now would be such a pity.

> *Leaving* home can be very traumatic.

> *Left* to himself, Paul copes quite well.

> *Having* left school at 15, David spent years without a job.

In a non-finite verb phrase, all the verbs have a non-finite form. The distinction between finite and non-finite verb phrases is important in the classification of clauses (▶see **4.2**).

3.3.5 │ Aspect

Tense (▶see **3.3.3**) refers to the absolute location of an event in time – either past or present. **Aspect** refers to how an event is to be viewed with respect to time. We can illustrate this using the following examples:

> [1] David fell in love on his eighteenth birthday.

> [2] David has fallen in love.

> [3] David is falling in love.

In [1], the verb *fell* tells us that David fell in love in the past, and specifically on his eighteenth birthday. This is a past-tense verb.

In [2] also, the action took place in the past, but it is implied that it took place quite recently. It is further implied that David's falling in love is still relevant at the time of speaking – *David has fallen in love, and that's why he's behaving so strangely now.*

The auxiliary *has* in [2] is the perfective auxiliary (▶see **2.7.5**), and it expresses **perfective aspect** in the verb phrase *has fallen*.

In [3], the action of falling in love is still in progress – David is falling in love at the time of speaking. For this reason, it is called **progressive aspect**. Progressive aspect is expressed by using the progressive auxiliary *be* (▶see **2.7.4**).

Aspect always includes tense. In [2] and [3] above, the verb phrases are in the present tense, but they could also be in the past tense:

> **Perfective aspect, past tense:**   David *had fallen* in love.
>
> **Progressive aspect, past tense:**   David *was falling* in love.

3.3.6 | Mood

Mood refers to distinctions in the form of a verb phrase that express the speaker's attitude towards what is said. There are three moods: indicative, imperative and subjunctive.

1   **Indicative** mood is the most common mood in declarative, interrogative and exclamative sentences (▶see **1.14**):

> Paul *enrolled* in a music class
>
> *Does* Amy *like* her new school?
>
> What a big house you *have*!

2   The **imperative** is used in issuing orders:

> *Move* over.
>
> *Stop* that at once.

3   **Subjunctive** mood is used when we refer to a non-factual or hypothetical situation:

> If I *were* you, I would accept the offer.

> If Mr Heseltine *were* Prime Minister, what would he do?

This is called the **were-subjunctive** because the verb phrase consists solely of *were*.

The **mandative subjunctive** is used after a small number of verbs, including *ask*, *decide*, *insist*, *recommend*, *suggest*, when these verbs are followed by *that*:

> The committee insisted that she *resign* immediately.

> The lawyer asked that he *be* given more time to prepare.

The mandative subjunctive is also used after the following adjectives: *crucial*, *essential*, *imperative*, *important*, *necessary*, *vital*:

> It is important that every room *be* ventilated.

> It is vital that prisoners *be* supervised at all times.

The use of the subjunctive is much more common in American English than in British English. In British English, the indicative mood is often preferred:

> If I *was* you, I would accept the offer.

> It is vital that prisoners *are* supervised at all times.

The subjunctive survives in a number of formulaic expressions:

> as it *were*

> *be* that as it may

> far *be* it from me

if need *be*

God *be* praised

long *live* the Queen

wish you *were* here

3.4 Adjective phrases

Adjective phrases have the following basic structure:

Premodifier	Adjective	Postmodifier
very	*reluctant*	to leave

The premodifier in an adjective phrase is most commonly an intensifier
(▶see **2.5.3**):

very useful

extremely cold

wonderfully creative

In expressions of measurement and age, a noun phrase may function as
a premodifier in an adjective phrase:

three months old

a metre long

10 mm wide

Postmodifiers occur after the adjective:

glad *you could come*

guilty *of murder*

reluctant *to leave*

happy *to oblige*

delighted *to meet you*

3.4.1 | *The functions of adjective phrases*

The major functions of adjective phrases are:

1   Subject complement (▶see **1.5**):

> Our aunt is *quite ill.*

> You were *very lucky.*

> My old teacher seemed *genuinely happy to see me.*

2   Premodifier of a noun (▶see **3.2.2**):

> Emily was wearing a *very old* dress.

> I've used a *slightly different* recipe this time.

> She's a *rather boring* person.

3   Object complement (▶see **1.8**):

> Ice cream always makes Simon *ill.*

> The new wallpaper makes the room *much brighter.*

> The Gulf Stream keeps our climate *fairly mild.*

3.5 Adverb phrases

Adverb phrases have the following basic structure:

Premodifier	Adverb	Postmodifier
very	*quickly*	indeed

The premodifier in an adverb phrase is always an intensifier (▶see **2.5.3**):

Premodifier	Adverb
very	gradually
too	slowly
extremely	badly
quite	soon

Postmodifiers in adverb phrases are quite rare. Apart from *indeed*, only *enough* is commonly used:

funnily *enough*   oddly *enough*

naturally *enough*   strangely *enough*

3.5.1 *The functions of adverb phrases*

The major functions of adverb phrases are:

1   Premodifier of an adjective (▶see **2.4**):

David is *extremely* sensitive.

Titanic was a *very* successful film.

The meat was *far too* salty.

2   Premodifier of an adverb (▶see **2.5**):

> I spoke to John *very* recently.

> She drives *far too* slowly.

> The other witness saw the incident *slightly more* clearly.

3   Adjunct (▶see **1.11**):

> *Suddenly* the factory closed and 200 jobs were lost.

> Full-time students receive a medical card *automatically*.

> He died in his forties *quite recently*.

3.6   Prepositional phrases

Prepositional phrases have the following basic structure:

Premodifier	Preposition	Complement
just	*after*	the game

The complement in a prepositional phrase is most commonly a noun phrase:

> in *London*

> around *the world*

> across *our street*

> through *the open window*

Clauses (▶see **4.3**) can also function as the complement in a prepositional phrase:

> It's a good way of *reducing the debt*.

> He succeeded by *working hard*.

Prepositional phrases usually consist of a preposition followed by its complement. Premodifiers in a prepositional phrase are quite rare, but here are some examples:

just after the game

straight across the road

right around the building

3.6.1 | The functions of prepositional phrases

The major functions of prepositional phrases are:

1   Postmodifier of a noun (▶see **3.2.3**):

The population *of China* is growing.

The demand *for British steel* has dropped dramatically.

Caroline is reading a book *on Renaissance painting*.

2   Adjunct (▶see **1.11**):

I've got to see the doctor *on Wednesday*.

Before the war, he played football for Leeds United.

We met David *beside the river*.

3   Subject complement (▶see **1.5**):

Your lunch is *in the microwave*.

The other gift is *for James*.

Phil Collins was *with a band called Genesis*.

4 Postmodifier of an adjective (▶see **3.4**):

Sarah is very proud *of her achievements.*

The villagers are not very tolerant *of strangers.*

The officers were found guilty *of disreputable conduct.*

5 Object complement (▶see **1.8**):

Sue has a job putting cards *in alphabetical order.*

I am obliged to place these matters *before the jury.*

She's got a drawing board *on her knee.*

Chapter 4

Sentences and clauses

This chapter covers three broad areas: **subordination** and **coordination** (▶see **4.1–4.10**); **linking sentences** (▶see **4.11–4.15**); and **focusing** and **emphasizing** (▶see **4.16–4.19**).

4.1 Complex sentences

In Chapter 1 we looked at the simple sentence *Paul plays football*, and we analysed it in terms of the following sentence elements: subject (S), verb (V) and direct object (DO):

S	V	DO
Paul	plays	football.

We also looked briefly at the following sentence:

When the plane landed, the ground crew removed the cargo.

We can analyse this sentence in the same way, in terms of the following sentence elements: adjunct (A), subject (S), verb (V) and direct object (DO):

A	S	V	DO
When the plane landed	the ground crew	removed	the cargo.

However, unlike the simple sentence, this sentence can be analysed further. This is because the adjunct (A) *when the plane landed* is itself a 'sentence-like' construction. It has its own subject, *the plane*, and its own verb, *landed*. So it displays the sentence pattern S+V. It also has an important additional element: it is introduced by the subordinating conjunction *when* (▶see **2.9**).

The presence of the subordinating conjunction indicates that *when the plane landed* is not an independent sentence. It is certainly 'sentence-like', since it displays the sentence pattern S+V, but it cannot stand alone. For this reason, we say that *when the plane landed* is a **subordinate clause**, not a sentence.

A subordinate clause such as *when the plane landed* is a dependent clause – it is part of a larger structure, usually a sentence. In contrast, *the ground crew removed the cargo* can stand alone – it is not subordinate to any higher structure.

A sentence which contains a subordinate clause is called a complex sentence.

4.2 Markers of subordination

There are two main indicators that a clause is subordinate:

1 **The presence of a subordinating conjunction.** Clauses which are introduced by one of the subordinating conjunctions (▶see **2.9**) are subordinate clauses. Here are some examples:

> James left the room *because he was angry.*

> *If you need more money,* just phone me.

> I read a magazine *while I was waiting.*

However, not all subordinate clauses are introduced by a subordinator. The subordinator *that*, for instance, may be omitted:

[1]   Paul knows *that Amy prefers tennis*.

[2]   Paul knows *Amy prefers tennis*.

In [1] *that* indicates that the clause *that Amy prefers tennis* is subordinate. In [2], however, there is no formal marker of subordination, though the clause *Amy prefers tennis* is still a subordinate clause. So while a subordinator always indicates a subordinate clause, not all subordinate clauses are introduced by a subordinator.

2   **The form of the verb phrase**. If the verb phrase is non-finite (▶see **3.3.4**), then the clause in which it occurs is a subordinate clause.

We recall that the non-finite verb forms are (1) the base form (often with *to*), (2) the *-ed* form and (3) the *-ing* form.

These three verb forms give their names to three subordinate clause types:

to-clauses

The road was widened *to improve the traffic flow*.

To receive all the channels, you may need an antenna.

A satellite must reach an altitude of 100 miles *to get clear of the atmosphere*.

-ed clauses

Deprived of oxygen, plants will quickly die.

The warriors faced each other, *dressed in black armour*.

Designed for drafting, mechanical pencils are also useful for sketching.

-ing clauses

Michelangelo painted *lying on his back*.

The teacher stood in the doorway, *saying nothing*.

Emily rang the doorbell, *her heart pounding*.

In a *to*-clause, *to* sometimes occurs as *in order to* or *so as to*:

> *In order to reduce heat loss*, we've sealed the window frames.

> Be punctual *so as to reduce waiting time*.

The form of the verb phrase, then, is a marker of subordination. If the verb phrase is non-finite, the clause which contains it is a subordinate clause.

4.3   Subordinate clause types

The main subordinate clause types are **adjunct clauses** (▶see **4.3.1**), **relative clauses** (▶see **4.3.2**), **nominal relative clauses** (▶see **4.3.3**), ***that*-clauses** (▶see **4.3.4**) and **comparative clauses** (▶see **4.3.5**).

4.3.1   Adjunct clauses

Adjunct clauses are subordinate clauses that function as adjuncts in sentence structure (▶see **1.11**). They are introduced by a wide range of subordinating conjunctions, including *although*, *because*, *if*, *since*, *when*, *while*:

> *Although he is only 18*, he has a very mature attitude.

> Sandra left early *because she has an interview tomorrow*.

> *If you don't hurry* you'll miss your flight.

> He's lived in the same house *since he was a boy*.

> *When he was young*, Van Gogh loved to paint trees.

> I'll watch a video *while you're out*.

Adjunct clauses express a very wide range of meanings (▶see **4.6**).

4.3.2 | Relative clauses

A relative clause is introduced by one of the relative pronouns, *that*, *who*, *which* or *whose* (▶see **2.6.6**):

> The book *that I am reading* is fascinating.

> The man *who lives beside us* is unwell.

> This is a company *which does not exclude people*.

> I've got a friend *whose parents are divorced*.

In some circumstances, the relative pronoun may be omitted, leaving a **zero relative clause**:

> The book *I am reading* is fascinating.
> (cf. The book *that I am reading* . . .)

In another variant, the relative pronoun is again omitted, and the verb has an *-ed* form or an *-ing* form (▶see **2.3.1**). This is a **reduced relative clause**:

> Houses *built in the 1940s* are usually draughty.
> (cf. Houses *which were built in the 1940s* . . .)

> The train *arriving at Platform One* is the Cambridge train.
> (cf. The train *which is arriving at Platform One* . . .)

4.3.3 | Nominal relative clauses

A nominal relative clause is introduced by *what*, *whatever*, *whoever*, *where* or *how*:

> *What you need* is a long holiday.

> Take *whatever you want*.

> *Whoever wins the most seats* will form a government.

This is *where the rebellion started.*

Laura showed me *how to set the timer.*

There is a close correspondence between a nominal relative clause and a noun phrase (▶see **3.2**):

What you need is a long holiday.

~*The thing that you need* is a long holiday.

Whoever wins the most seats will form a government.

~*The party that wins the most seats* will form a government.

Laura showed me *how to set the timer.*

~Laura showed me *the way to set the timer.*

| 4.3.4 | **That-*clauses***

A *that*-clause is introduced by the subordinating conjunction *that*:

Everyone knows *that smoking is dangerous.*

The new ruling means *that pensioners will suffer.*

Bernard has decided *that he wants to live in Canada.*

It is important to distinguish clearly between the subordinating conjunction *that* and the relative pronoun *that*. Relative pronoun *that* introduces a relative clause, and it can usually be replaced by *which*:

The book *that I am reading* is fascinating.

~The book *which I am reading* is fascinating.

In contrast, the subordinating conjunction *that* cannot be replaced by *which*:

Everyone knows *that smoking is dangerous.*

*~Everyone knows *which smoking is dangerous.*

| 4.3.5 | *Comparative clauses* |

Comparative clauses are introduced by *than* or *as*. Clauses introduced by *than* express comparison in a gradable adjective or adverb:

Mary is older *than I am.*

It travels faster *than you'd expect.*

Everything is more expensive *than it used to be.*

Comparative clauses introduced by *as* express equivalence:

Mary is as old *as I am.*

This is as good *as it gets.*

You can be as personal *as you like.*

4.4 Clauses as sentence elements

As elements in sentence structure, subordinate clauses most commonly function as adjuncts (▶see 1.11). They may also have the following functions:

1 **Subject** (▶see 1.2):

What you need is a long holiday.	nominal relative
Leaving home can be very traumatic.	*-ing* clause
To give up now would be such a pity.	*to*-clause
That he should fail to turn up is really annoying.	*that*-clause

With the exception of nominal relatives and *-ing* clauses, clauses functioning as subjects are rare. The *-ed* type (*Dressed in armour . . .*) cannot function as a subject.

▶See also **Postponed subjects, 4.18**.

2   **Direct object** (▶see 1.6):

Paul knows *that Amy prefers tennis.*   *that*-clause

Jim offered *to drive us to the airport.*   *to*-clause

Mary enjoys *visiting art galleries.*   *-ing* clause

We still don't know *what will happen.*   nominal relative

3   **Subject complement** (▶see 1.5):

A detective's first job is *to collect the evidence.*   *to*-clause

The main problem is *finding enough money.*   *-ing* clause

The real reason is *that I can't stand him.*   *that*-clause

That's *what I'm trying to tell you.*   nominal relative

4.5   Clauses as phrase elements

When a subordinate clause occurs as an element in a phrase, it most commonly functions as a postmodifier. Subordinate clauses may occur as postmodifiers in the following phrase types (the phrases are bracketed).

1   Postmodifier in a noun phrase (▶see 3.2.3):

[The man *who lives beside us*] is unwell.   relative clause

[The man *to ask about plumbing*] is Mr Davis   *to*-clause

That-clauses function as complements in noun phrases (▶see 3.2.5):

[The fact *that no one came*] is really disappointing.

[The news *that everyone on board was killed*] has just reached us.

2   Postmodifier in an adjective phrase (▶see **3.4**):

    I wasn't [aware *that I had to register.*]   *that*-clause

    Chelsea were [reluctant *to admit defeat.*]   *to*-clause

3   Complement in a prepositional phrase (▶see **3.6**):

    She has a reputation [for *being difficult.*]   *-ing* clause

    He's still coming to terms [with *what happened.*] nominal relative

4.6   The meanings of adjunct clauses

For the meanings expressed by adjuncts in a sentence, ▶see **1.12**. We identified three main types of meaning: manner, time and place. However, when clauses function as adjuncts, they can express a much wider range of meanings. The main types of meaning expressed by adjunct clauses are shown here:

Time:

    I'll speak to you again *before you leave.*

    When you leave, please close the door.

    I'll read the newspaper *while I'm waiting.*

Condition:

    I'll be home early *if I can catch the early train.*

    Provided he works hard, he'll do very well at school.

    Don't call me *unless it's an emergency.*

Concession:

    He paid for the meal, *although he can't really afford it.*

    Even though he worked hard, he failed the final exam.

    While I don't agree with her, I can see why she's angry.

Reason:

> Bernard was an hour late *because he missed his train.*
>
> I borrowed your laptop, *since you weren't using it.*
>
> *As I don't know the way,* I'll take a taxi.

Result:

> The kitchen was flooded, *so we had to go to a restaurant.*
>
> I've forgotten my password, *so I can't read my e-mail.*
>
> Hamilton lost the case, *so he had to pay all the costs.*

Purpose:

> Leave a window open *to let the steam out.*
>
> *In order to meet growing demand,* the BBC introduced a new service in the UHF part of the spectrum.
>
> You should write down the number *so you won't forget it.*

The type of meaning expressed by an adjunct clause is often predictable from the subordinating conjunction which introduces it. For instance, *if* always introduces a **conditional clause**, and *because* always introduces a reason clause.

However, some subordinating conjunctions can introduce more than one type. *While* can introduce a clause expressing time (*I'll read the newspaper **while I'm waiting***) as well as a clause expressing concession (***While I don't agree with her,** I can see why she's angry*). Similarly, *since* can express time (*He's lived there **since he was a boy***) as well as reason (***Since you can't drive,** you'll have to take a taxi*).

4.7 Peripheral clauses

In this section we look briefly at a range of clause types which are peripheral in sentence structure. These peripheral clauses are grammatically unintegrated, to varying degrees, in the sentences that contain them.

4.7.1 | Comment clauses

A **comment clause** is a brief clause inserted into a sentence, expressing the speaker's attitude towards what is being said:

> We could, *I suppose*, share one between us.
>
> So the building was used, *I imagine*, for storing grain.
>
> She was acting on impulse, *I guess*.
>
> I can't help you, *I'm afraid*.

Other comment clauses include: *I assume, I reckon, I should think, I must say, I'm sorry to say, I must admit*.

4.7.2 | Reporting clauses and direct speech

A **reporting clause** identifies the speaker of direct speech:

> 'The music is too loud,' *said Jim*.
>
> *The lady said*, 'I don't need any help'.

In **direct speech**, the exact words used by a speaker are quoted, as in these examples. In **indirect speech**, the words are subsequently reported by someone else:

Direct speech: 'The music is too loud', said Jim.

Indirect speech: Jim said that the music was too loud.

The switch from direct speech to indirect speech involves a change of tense. Here, the present tense verb (*is*) in direct speech becomes the past tense verb (*was*) in indirect speech.

Reporting clauses are often extended by the use of adjuncts (►see 1.11):

> 'The music is too loud', said Jim *angrily*.
>
> 'It's a wonderful gift', said Laura *gratefully*.
>
> 'I'm not coming back', cried Tom, *as he slammed the door*.

4.7.3 | Tag questions

Particularly in spoken English, questions are often added to the end of a declarative sentence (►see 1.14.1):

> You were born in London, *weren't you?*

The interrogative *weren't you?* is called a **tag question**, because it is 'tagged on' to the end of the declarative *You were born in London*. Tag questions are used to seek agreement with what has just been said in the declarative part. Further examples include:

> It's very warm, *isn't it?*

> The policy hasn't really worked, *has it?*

> Bernard worked in Whitehall, *didn't he?*

4.7.4 | Parentheticals

A **parenthetical** is a complete sentence which is inserted 'parenthetically' into another sentence. In writing, parentheticals are marked off from the main sentence by enclosing them in brackets or dashes:

> The range of colours (*most suppliers have* 72) can include metallics, and both warm and cool greys.

> By Bugatti standards it was not technically advanced – *smaller Bugattis used similar technical layouts* – merely bigger and grander, in all respects.

A parenthetical sentence has no grammatical connection with the main sentence. In speech, parentheticals are sometimes introduced by *and*:

> There is a sense in which *and Hogarth realized this* satire is also a form of entertainment.

4.7.5 | *Sentential relative clauses*

A **sentential relative clause** is introduced by the relative pronoun *which*. Sentential relatives are used to add a comment about what has just been said:

> James took the early train, *which was lucky for him.*

> Mary finally passed her exams, *which was a relief to everyone.*

> John doesn't want to meet Laura, *which I can understand.*

4.8 Coordination

Coordination links items of 'equal' grammatical status. In the following examples the coordinated items are italicised:

[1]   *Anthony* and *Caroline* have arrived.

[2]   She bought *a new dress* and *a handbag.*

[3]   The house was *old* and *damp.*

[4]   Simon writes *clearly* and *legibly.*

Sentences [1] and [2] illustrate the coordination of noun phrases (▶see **3.2**). Sentence [3] involves coordination of adjective phrases (▶see **3.4**), and sentence [4] involves coordination of adverb phrases (▶see **3.5**).

Coordination can also be used to link clauses:

> *David drinks milk* and *I drink beer.*

> *The deception was uncovered* and *the minister resigned.*

> *The hotel was lovely* but *the weather was awful.*

Finally, parts of clauses may be coordinated. The following examples show the coordination of predicates (▶see **1.2**):

James quit his job and *went to live in Scotland.*

The plane took off but *never reached its destination.*

4.9 Coordination types

Coordination normally uses one of the coordinating conjunctions *and*, *but* or *or* to create a link between items:

Quickly *and* resolutely, he strode into the bank.

The course was short *but* intensive.

I don't like laziness *or* dishonesty.

This type of coordination, with a coordinating conjunction actually present, is called **syndetic coordination**.

Coordination can also occur without a coordinating conjunction, as in:

Quickly, resolutely, he strode into the bank.

Coordination without the use of a coordinating conjunction is called **asyndetic coordination**.

When three or more items are coordinated, the coordinating conjunction is usually placed between the final two items only:

We need bread, cheese, eggs, flour *and* milk.

This is syndetic coordination, since a coordinating conjunction, *and*, is present. It would be unusual to find a coordinating conjunction between each item:

We need bread *and* cheese *and* eggs *and* flour *and* milk.

This is called **polysyndetic coordination**. It is usually only used for effect, for instance, to express repetition or continuation:

He just talks *and* talks *and* talks.

I've said it again *and* again *and* again.

This play will run *and* run *and* run.

The coordinators *and* and *or* can be used to link any number of items in coordination. However, *but* is slightly different. It can link a maximum of two items, usually clauses:

Steve Cram ran well *but* he was overtaken in the last length.

4.10 Pseudo-coordination

The coordinators *and* and *or* are sometimes used when no real coordination is taking place:

I'll be there when I'm good *and* ready.

Here, *and* does not coordinate *good* with *ready*. If it did, the sentence would mean something like: *I'll be there when I'm good **and when I'm ready**.* Instead, it means *I'll be there when I'm **fully/completely** ready.*

This use of *and* without any coordinating role is called **pseudo-coordination**. Further examples of pseudo-coordination include:

Please try *and* come early.
(= Please try to come early.)

Any more complaints *and* I'm leaving.
(= If I receive any more complaints, I will leave.)

Do that again *and* I'll report you.
(= If you do that again, I will report you.)

When it acts as a coordinator, the conjunction *or* links items which are to be considered as alternatives:

Would you like tea *or* coffee?

You can fly business class *or* economy class.

In the following example, however, the items linked by *or* are not alternatives:

The software is supplied with several useful 'wizards' *or* templates.

Here, *templates* is used to clarify the specialist computer term *wizards*, so this is a type of apposition (▶see **3.2.6**).

4.11 Sentence connectors

Throughout this book we have taken the sentence as the largest grammatical unit. However, in all forms of continuous communication, both spoken and written, sentences do not operate independently of each other. Instead, effective communication depends to a very large extent on placing sentences in the correct sequence, and on creating meaningful links between them. In this section we look at some grammatical devices which enable us to create links between sentences in discourse.

There are two main types of sentence connectors: logical connectors (▶see **4.11.1**) and structural connectors (▶see **4.11.2**).

4.11.1 | Logical connectors

Logical connectors express a logical relationship between sentences. They express two main types of relationship:

1   **Contrast/concession**. Contrast/concession connectors are used to express a contrast between the information expressed by two sentences:

> The closing date for the receipt of applications is 15 December. *However,* students are advised to submit their applications as soon as possible after 1 September.

> It was already clear yesterday that Moscow was losing hope it could persuade the United States and its allies to hold off a ground war for much longer. *Nevertheless,* the Soviet president continued his campaign of high-level diplomacy.

> Anybody who says that there is great glory in war is off his head. *On the other hand,* I have to say that war does bring out in people extraordinary nobility [. . .]

Other contrast/concession connectors include: *alternatively, anyway, besides, instead, nonetheless, still, yet.*

2   **Result**. Result connectors are used to indicate that the second sentence expresses the result or consequence of what has gone before:

> Approval has already been given for a golf course at Smithstown, only three miles away. *Therefore*, an extra facility in the area was considered to be unnecessary.

> I have not yet issued you with an invoice for the period prior to Christmas. *Consequently*, I am enclosing an invoice for the total amount of time used so far.

> Thousands of commuters have been evacuated from platforms as the police launch a full-scale search. *As a result*, all underground stations with connections to British Rail are also shut.

Other result connectors include: *accordingly*, *hence*, *in consequence*, *so*, *then*, *thus*.

4.11.2 *Structural connectors*

Structural connectors are devices for ordering sentences, and for organizing the points we wish to make. Structural connectors are used for the following purposes:

1   **Listing**. Listing connectors are used to list points in a specific order:

> *First*, he cannot stand against the leader unless he is fairly sure of a victory [. . .] But *second*, and more important, should the Tories lose the next election he will be damned and written out of the succession [. . .]

> *Firstly* you have your brakes [. . .] *Secondly* you've got the throttle here on the handlebars.

> *To begin with*, turn down the colour control until you have a black and white image [. . .] *then* manipulate the contrast and brightness controls [. . .]

Other listing connectors include: *in the first place, in the second place, for one thing, for another thing, finally, lastly*.

2 **Adding**. Adding connectors are used to add new pieces of information to what has previously been said:

> Without such disclosure any consent received would not be informed or valid. *In addition*, the doctor would be in breach of his duty.

> Now there are fewer than 50 goats that have to share the island with 85,000 land-hungry people. *Furthermore*, it is almost impossible to guarantee their protection.

> As I had known Michael, Sarah and Victoria from their childhood [...] this remark came as rather a shock. *Also*, I was baffled by the logic.

Other adding connectors include: *additionally, moreover, what is more, on top of that* (informal), *as well as that*.

3 **Summing up**. 'Summing up' connectors are used to introduce a section which 'sums up' or concludes what has gone before:

> *To conclude*: the fear of an overwhelming burden of old people is one of the least defensible arguments [...]

> *In sum*, everything concerning the size, population, institutions, and requirements of an imperial capital are inflated [...]

> *All in all*, he felt he'd had enough.

Other 'summing up' connectors include: *altogether, in conclusion, in summary, overall, to summarize*.

4 **Exemplifying**. Exemplifying connectors introduce examples or instances in support of what has previously been said:

> For this reason, quite serious injuries may not be investigated. *For example*, finger amputations may be overlooked.

Ultraviolet radiation is known to have effects on the immune system. *For instance*, coldsores not infrequently occur at the beginning of a summer holiday.

The reverse case also existed. *That is*, circumstances in which words derived from the holy tongue were to be avoided.

Other exemplifying connectors include: *e.g.* (= *for example*), *i.e* (= *that is*), *namely*.

4.12   Expressing point of view

Writers can introduce their own point of view very directly by using one of the following:

in my opinion

in my view

as I see it

if you ask me (informal)

In addition, certain adverbs can express the writer's point of view. Usually, an adverb at the start of a sentence describes the action of the verb:

[1]   *Gradually*, the swelling will disappear.

This can be paraphrased as: *The swelling will disappear **in a gradual manner***.

Compare this with:

[2]   *Hopefully*, the swelling will disappear.

This cannot be paraphrased as *The swelling will disappear **in a hopeful manner***. Instead, *hopefully* here expresses the speaker's attitude towards what is being said. So we might paraphrase [2] as: *I hope that the swelling will disappear*.

The italicized adverbs in the following examples also express point of view:

> Vincent Van Gogh arrived at the end of the last century to paint his vivid and expressive pictures telling us of his love for the place. *Sadly*, too much sunshine and far too much alcohol got the better of him.

> The air mass bringing the coldest temperatures is the polar continental mass, which comes in from the Soviet Union. *Fortunately*, it is not that common.

> The painting was stolen on Sunday night. *Surprisingly*, no one realized it was missing until Wednesday.

> This should have been part of the vision of the new British Steel. *Regrettably*, it wasn't.

Other point-of-view adverbs include: *curiously, frankly, funnily (enough), honestly, ironically, luckily, oddly (enough), predictably, presumably, wisely.*

4.13 Referring expressions

Continuous discourse always contains a great deal of cross-referring from one part of the text to another. In fact, the coherence of a text – whether written or spoken – depends on making unambiguous cross-references between the various parts. To give a simple example:

> *Simon* came home early. *He* was not feeling well.

Here, the personal pronoun *he* refers back to the proper noun *Simon*. The pronoun creates a simple, unambiguous connection between the two sentences. Referring back in this way is called anaphoric reference, or simply **anaphora**. The item that is referred back to is called the **antecedent**. So in this example, *Simon* is the antecedent of *he*.

Using pronouns is the most common way to make cross-references in a text. The following examples illustrate the use of pronouns to refer back. In each example, the antecedent and its corresponding pronoun are shown in italic.

You should prepare *a study timetable*. You can modify *it* later if you need to.

I like *Juliet Stephenson*. I saw *her* in Truly Madly Deeply.

London Underground has announced *the suspension of trains on the Circle Line*. *This* is due to track maintenance work.

When we feel emotion, *certain involuntary changes* occur within us. *These* include changes in salivation, breathing, and heart-rate.

A pronoun can also refer back to the whole of a previous sentence:

Check-in time was ten o'clock. That meant we had to get up at six.

Referring back is the most common type of cross-referencing in a text. However, we can also refer forward:

It's here at last. *The new Nissan Micra* was launched this week.

Referring forward is called cataphoric reference, or **cataphora**.

4.14 Antecedent agreement

In the sentences

Simon came home early. He was not feeling well.

we say that *Simon* is the antecedent of *he* (►see **4.13**). The pronoun *he* agrees with its antecedent in number (singular), person (third) and gender (masculine). This is called **antecedent agreement**.

For the purposes of clear communication, it is important to ensure that there is agreement between a pronoun and its antecedent. In the following, there is no agreement:

A good speaker system can be all that's needed to transform your PC from a piece of furniture into an entertainment centre. *They* can give games a lift as much as any posh graphics card.

Since the antecedent *a good speaker system* is singular, we would expect the singular pronoun *it* in the second sentence: **It** *can give games a lift . . .*

Perhaps more importantly for clear communication, the antecedent should be unambiguous:

> Laura used to babysit a little girl who kept throwing *her* shoes in the fire.

Here, the antecedent of *her* is ambiguous. Whose shoes were thrown in the fire, Laura's or the little girl's? In grammatical terms, is *Laura* or *a little girl* the antecedent of *her*?

4.15   Substitution using *so* and *do*

The word *so* can be used as a substitute for an entire previous sentence:

> Q.   Will we have time for breakfast at the airport?
>
> A.   I hope *so*.
>   (= I hope we will have time for breakfast at the airport.)

Using *so* in this way means that we can avoid unwieldy repetition.

The negative counterpart of *so* is *not*:

> Q.   Is Jim coming tonight?
>
> A.   I hope *not*.
>   (= I hope Jim is not coming tonight.)

So can also substitute for a phrase:

> The meat was very fresh and *so* were the vegetables.

Here, *so* substitutes for the adjective phrase *very fresh*. The negative counterpart of phrasal *so* is *neither*:

> The meat was not very fresh and *neither* were the vegetables.

The verb *do* can also be used as a substitute:

> They asked me to drive them to the airport and I *did*.

Do sometimes combines with *so* as a substitute:

> You should save a little money every month. If you *do so*, you will have no worries.

Here, *do so* substitutes for *save a little money every month*.

4.16 Fronting

Fronting occurs when we move one of the sentence elements from its usual position to the beginning of the sentence. Consider the following simple sentence:

> David (S) owes (V) £4000 (DO).

The direct object *£4000* can be 'fronted' as follows:

> £4000 (DO) David (S) owes (V).

Fronting gives special emphasis to the fronted element. In this example, it might be used to express astonishment at the amount of money that David owes. The following examples also contain fronted direct objects:

> *Ice-cream* he wants! (cf. He wants *ice-cream*.)

> *Some games* we won easily. (cf. We won *some games* easily.)

> *That much* I understand. (cf. I understand *that much*.)

A subject complement (▶see 1.5) may also be fronted:

> *Stone cold* her hands were. (cf. Her hands were *stone cold*.)

> *Extremely rude* she was. (cf. She was *extremely rude*.)

4.17 Cleft sentences

The simple sentence *Simon studied French last year* can be rewritten as:

It was Simon who studied French last year.

This is called a **cleft sentence** because the original simple sentence has been divided (or 'cleft') into two clauses:

Clause 1: *It was Simon*

Clause 2: *who studied French last year*

A cleft sentence is used when we wish to emphasize one element of the original sentence, often as a way of excluding other possibilities:

It was *Simon* who studied French last year (not *Amy*).

Here, *Simon*, the subject of the original sentence, is emphasized. We can also emphasize other elements, including the direct object *French*:

It was *French* that Simon studied last year (not *German*).

Finally, we can emphasize the adjunct *last year*:

It was *last year* that Simon studied French (not *this year*).

The emphasized element in a cleft sentence is called the **focus**. Cleft sentences are introduced by *it*, and the verb is always *be*. Therefore the pattern of a cleft sentence is:

It	*Be*	Focus	Clause
It	was	Simon	who studied French last year.

4.18   Postponed subjects

The subject is usually the first element in a sentence. However, if the subject is a clause, it may be postponed to the end:

It's not surprising *that James failed his exams.*

Here, the subject is the *that*-clause *that James failed his exams.* The subject has been postponed to the end of the sentence, and its normal position is filled by *it.* In the more typical pattern, with the subject at the beginning, this sentence sounds stylistically awkward:

That James failed his exams is not surprising.

To-clauses may be postponed in the same way:

It was a good idea *to bring an umbrella.*
(cf. *To bring an umbrella* was a good idea.)

It is particularly desirable to postpone a subject clause when it is very long:

It soon came to our attention *that no one from the area had actually applied for any type of housing benefit.*
(cf. *That no one from the area had actually applied for any type of housing benefit* soon came to our attention.)

Postponing the subject is not always just a matter of style. With some verbs, postponement is obligatory:

It seems *that many people are deeply attached to the monarchy.*
~That many people are deeply attached to the monarchy seems.

It appears *that his statement had wider implications.*
~That his statement had wider implications appears.

It turned out *that his secretary had stolen the money.*
~That his secretary had stolen the money turned out.

4.19 **There-sentences**

There-sentences are introduced by the word *there*:

> *There* is a man at the door.

> *There* is a God after all.

> *There* was a phonecall for you.

> *There* is no such thing as a popular tax.

There-sentences are chiefly used to introduce new information relating to the existence – or non-existence – of some state of affairs. For this reason they are sometimes called 'existential' sentences.

The word *there* in these constructions should be distinguished from the adverb *there*, which denotes place:

> *There* he is. (cf. He is *there*.)

Chapter 5

Word formation and spelling

5.1　The structure of words

Many words in English have a recognisable internal structure. For example, the word *unsuccessful* can be broken down into the following three parts:

un + success + ful

The first part, *un-*, is called the **prefix**. The second part – *success* – is a complete word in itself, and is called the **base**. The last part, *-ful*, is called the **suffix**.

Prefix	Base	Suffix
un	success	ful

Prefixes and suffixes are added to existing words to create new words.

5.2　Prefixes

Prefixes are added to the beginning of a word to create a new word. They contribute specific types of meaning. For instance, when we add the prefix *pre-* to the word *1945*, we create a new word *pre-1945*, meaning *before* 1945. The following are the main prefixes used in English, together with the kinds of meaning they contribute.

anti-
against, opposed to   *anti-depressant, anti-nuclear, anti-war, anti-Western*

de-
to reverse something   *decriminalise, de-activate, de-commission, deform*

dis-
reverse of   *disagreement, disapprove, dislike, disqualify,*
remove something   *disambiguate, disarm, disenfranchise, dislodge*

extra-
beyond   *extraterrestrial, extra-curricular, extra-mural, extra-sensory*

il-, im-, in-, ir-
not   *illegal, illegible, illegitimate, impatient, impossible, impolite, inappropriate, inconceivable, intolerant, irregular, irrelevant, irresponsible*

inter-
between   *international, inter-racial, intergalactic, interwoven*

mis-
to do something   *miscalculate, misconstrue, miskick,*
  badly or incorrectly   *misunderstand*

non-
not   *non-European, non-resident, non-stick, non-white*

post-
after   *post-1945, postgraduate, post-colonial, post-war*

pre-
before   *pre-1914, pre-war, predetermined, pre-set*

pro-
in favour of   *pro-life, pro-democracy, pro-Europe*

re-

to do something again *re-apply, re-design, re-introduce, repaint*

un-

reverse of   *unclear, undemocratic, unnecessary, unusual,*

remove something   *undress, unleash, unmask, unscrew*

5.3   Suffixes

Suffixes are added to the end of a word to create a new word. Certain suffixes are associated with certain word classes. For instance, the suffix *-able* appears at the end of many adjectives, including *reasonable, remarkable, believable*. The suffix *-ist* is used to create many nouns, including *capitalist, physicist, specialist*. The following are the most common suffixes associated with the major word classes.

1   Noun suffixes:

-age	*blockage, drainage, postage, spillage*
-al	*betrayal, dismissal, recital, removal*
-ant	*claimant, contestant, inhabitant, informant*
-dom	*freedom, kingdom, martyrdom, officialdom*
-ee	*absentee, employee, refugee, trainee*
-er/-or	*actor, blender, defender, eraser, teacher*
-ism	*ageism, favouritism, racism, terrorism*
-ist	*artist, cyclist, motorist, perfectionist*
-ity	*opportunity, publicity, responsibility, severity*
-ment	*embarrassment, environment, equipment, government*
-ness	*coolness, dryness, smoothness, willingness*
-ship	*citizenship, dictatorship, hardship, relationship*
-tion	*demonstration, ignition, migration, recreation*

2   Adjective suffixes:

-able	*achievable, profitable, reasonable, remarkable*
-al	*accidental, industrial, musical, physical, whimsical*
-ful	*grateful, hopeful, successful, tuneful, useful*
-ish	*amateurish, childish, feverish, foolish, ghoulish*
-less	*careless, homeless, hopeless, painless, restless*
-like	*apelike, childlike, godlike, starlike*
-y	*cloudy, creepy, funny, rainy, sleepy*

3   Verb suffixes:

-ate	*adjudicate, congratulate, hyphenate, populate*
-en	*broaden, deafen, ripen, sadden, tighten, widen*
-ify	*amplify, beautify, clarify, classify, identify, purify*
-ise/-ize	*economize, modernize, popularize, realise, terrorize*

4   Adverb suffixes:

-ly	*brilliantly, carefully, slowly, smoothly, terribly*
-wards	*afterwards, backwards, onwards, upwards*
-wise	*anticlockwise, clockwise, health-wise, relationship-wise*

5.4   Compounding and blending

Compounding involves combining two bases (▶see **5.1**) to create a new word. For instance, the bases *head* and *ache* combine to form *headache*. Further examples of compounding include:

chair + person	=	*chairperson*
green + house	=	*greenhouse*
help + line	=	*helpline*
key + board	=	*keyboard*
life + style	=	*lifestyle*
match + box	=	*matchbox*
news + paper	=	*newspaper*
post + card	=	*postcard*

Many adjectives are formed by compounding a noun with the *-ed* or *-ing* form of a verb (▶see 2.3.1), as set out below.

Noun		-ed/-ing Verb		Adjective
drug	+	induced	=	*drug-induced*
poverty	+	stricken	=	*poverty-stricken*
battery	+	operated	=	*battery-operated*
stress	+	related	=	*stress-related*
rat	+	infested	=	*rat-infested*
award	+	winning	=	*award-winning*
eye	+	catching	=	*eye-catching*
fun	+	loving	=	*fun-loving*
penny	+	pinching	=	*penny-pinching*
time	+	consuming	=	*time-consuming*

►See also **Participial adjectives** (**2.4.3**).

Blending is similar to compounding, except that only parts of existing words are combined to create a new word. For example, the word *camcorder* is formed by combining *cam* (from *camera*) with *corder* (from *recorder*). Other examples of blending include:

bionic	=	*bio*logical + electro*nic*
biopic	=	*bio*graphical + *pic*ture
Britpop	=	*Brit*ish *pop* music
docudrama	=	*docu*mentary + *drama*
docusoap	=	*docu*mentary + *soap* opera
ecoterrorism	=	*eco*logy + *terrorism*
edutainment	=	*edu*cation + enter*tainment*
Eurovision	=	*Euro*pean + tele*vision*
e-zine	=	*e*lectronic maga*zine*
heliport	=	*heli*copter + air*port*
infotainment	=	*info*rmation + enter*tainment*
motel	=	*mo*tor + ho*tel*
netiquette	=	I*net*rnet + e*tiquette*
netizen	=	I*net*rnet + ci*tizen*
paratroopers	=	*para*chute + *troopers*
pulsar	=	*pul*sating + st*ar*
smog	=	*sm*oke + f*og*

5.5 **Acronyms, abbreviations, and clipping**

5.5
Acronyms,
abbrevia-
tions, and
clipping

Acronyms are formed by combining the initial letters or syllables of two or more words. The combination is pronounced as a single word:

AIDS	acquired immune deficiency syndrome
BIOS	Basic Input Output System
DOS	Disk Operating System
FAQ	frequently asked questions
laser	light amplification by stimulated emission of radiation
Oxfam	Oxford Committee for Famine Relief
radar	radio detecting and ranging
RAM	random access memory
ROM	read-only memory
SAD	seasonal affective disorder
SALT	Strategic Arms Limitation Treaty
scuba	self-contained underwater breathing apparatus
UNPROFOR	United Nations Protection Force
WYSIWYG	What You See Is What You Get

Abbreviations are also formed from the initial letters of words, but unlike acronyms, they are spoken by spelling out each letter:

ATM	automated teller machine
BST	British Standard Time
cpu	central processing unit

DVD	digital video disk
EC	European Community
HTML	hypertext markup language
http	hypertext transfer protocol
ISD	international subscriber dialling
IT	information technology
o.g.	own goal
OTT	over the top
PC	personal computer (*also* political correctness)
PRP	performance-related pay (*also* profit-related pay)
RSI	repetitive strain injury
UFO	unidentified flying object
UNHCR	United Nations High Commission for Refugees
URL	Universal Resource Locator
VCR	video cassette recorder
WWW	World Wide Web

The following abbreviations are now widely used in e-mail messages and in online discussion groups:

AFK	away from keyboard
BTW	by the way
FWIW	for what it's worth
FYI	for your information

IMHO	in my humble opinion
IMO	in my opinion
LOL	laughing out loud

Clipping is a type of abbreviation in which one or more syllables are omitted or 'clipped' from a word. Most commonly, the beginning of the word is retained:

ad (or *advert*)	advertisement
decaff (also *decaf*)	decaffeinated coffee
demo	demonstration
exam	examination
improv	improvisation
lab	laboratory
memo	memorandum
movie	moving picture
photo	photograph
pub	public house

Clipping is a very common method of creating familiar personal names, including *Fred* (from *Frederick*), *Tim* (from *Timothy*) and *Seb* (from *Sebastian*).

5.6 Back formations

Back formations are words (usually verbs) formed by removing from a noun what is thought to be a suffix, and adding a verb ending. In the following, the right-hand column shows the word from which the back formation is derived.

emote	emotion
enthuse	enthusiasm
liaise	liaison
sculpt	sculptor
televise	television

The verb *legitimize* is formed by back formation from the adjective *legitimate*.

5.7 Combining forms

Combining forms are segments that do not exist as words in their own right. They are added to the beginning or end of another segment or word to create a new word. The following combining forms have been especially productive in recent years:

bio-	*biodiversity, bioethics, biohazard, biosphere*
cyber-	*cybernaut, cybernetics, cyberspace*
e-	*e-mail/email, e-business, e-commerce, e-text*
Euro-	*Eurocrat, Eurosceptic, Eurostar, Eurotunnel*
hyper-	*hyperlink, hypermarket, hypermedia, hypertext*
mega-	*megabucks, megabyte, megastar, megastore*
techno-	*technobabble, technocrat, technojunkie, techno-pop*
tele-	*telecottage, telematics, teleworking, telemarketing*
-ware	*freeware, groupware, hardware, shareware, software*

5.8   Inflections

Inflections are a special type of suffix (▶see **5.3**). They are added to the end of a word to indicate a grammatical property. For instance, the *-s* inflection is added to a noun to indicate plural number (*tree/trees*).

Inflections differ from other suffixes in one important respect. The suffix *-ment*, for example, added to the verb *embarrass* creates a completely different word, the noun *embarrassment*. Adding an inflection, however, does not create a new word, but a different grammatical form of the same word. For example, the words *tree* and *trees* are two forms of the same lexical word *tree*. In a dictionary, they would both appear under *tree*. They differ only in number: *tree* is singular and *trees* is plural.

In comparison with other languages, English has very few inflections. They are always suffixes, that is, they are always added to the end of a word. The inflections are shown in Table 3.

Table 3
Inflections

		Inflection	Examples
Nouns	Plural number	-s	trees
	Genitive	-'s	John's car
		-'	the boys' school
Main Verbs	-s form (3rd-person singular)	-s	walks
	past form	-ed	walked
	-ed form	-ed	walked
	-ing form	-ing	walking
Adjectives and adverbs	Comparative	-er	older, sooner
	Superlative	-est	oldest, soonest

5.9   **Adding inflections: general spelling rules**

There are four general spelling rules for adding inflections. These are set out below:

1   **Spelling rule 1**. Double the final consonant before adding *-ed*, *-ing*, *-er* or *-est*:

Verb	+-*ed*	+-*ing*
rub	rubbed	rubbing
stop	stopped	stopping
gag	gagged	gagging
jam	jammed	jamming
plan	planned	planning
occur	occurred	occurring
regret	regretted	regretting
Adjective	+-*er*	+-*est*
red	redder	reddest
big	bigger	biggest
grim	grimmer	grimmest
wet	wetter	wettest

5.9
Adding
inflections:
general
spelling
rules

- In British English, verbs ending in *-el* double the *l*:

travel	travelled	travelling
marvel	marvelled	marvelling

  However, in American English, final *l* is not doubled:

travel	traveled	traveling
marvel	marveled	marveling

- Final *l* is not doubled when it follows *a* or *o*:

conceal	concealed	concealing
reveal	revealed	revealing
cool	cooled	cooling

- Final *g* is not doubled when it follows *n*:

strong	stronger	strongest
young	younger	youngest

2 **Spelling rule 2**. Change final *y* to *i* before adding *-s*, *-ed*, *-er* or *-est*:

Verb	+-s	+-ed
cry	cries	cried
occupy	occupies	occupied
try	tries	tried
worry	worries	worried
Adjective	+-er	+-est
easy	easier	easiest

funny	funnier	funniest
heavy	heavier	heaviest
weary	wearier	weariest
Adverb	+-er	+-est
early	earlier	earliest

- If the final *y* follows a vowel, then it is retained:

convey	conveys	conveyed
delay	delays	delayed
play	plays	played
enjoy	enjoys	enjoyed

- The verbs *lay*, *pay*, and *say* do not take an *-ed* ending:

lay	lays	laid
pay	pays	paid
say	says	said

3 **Spelling rule 3**. Drop silent *e* before adding *-ed*, *-ing*, *-er*, or *-est*:

Verb	+-ed	+-ing
care	cared	caring
change	changed	changing
hope	hoped	hoping
love	loved	loving
Adjective	+-er	+-est
blue	bluer	bluest

5.9
Adding
inflections:
general
spelling
rules

close	closer	closest
large	larger	largest
whitest	whiter	whitest

- If the base ends in *ie*, change *ie* to *y* before adding *-ing*:

die	dying
lie	lying
tie	tying

- The *e* is retained in *dyeing* and *canoeing*.

4 **Spelling rule 4**. Add *e* before *-s* if the base ends in one of the following: *s*, *sh*, *ch*, *tch*, *x* or *z*:

Verb	+s
pass	passes
push	pushes
teach	teaches
catch	catches
relax	relaxes
buzz	buzzes
Noun	+s
mass	masses
box	boxes
church	churches
match	matches
wish	wishes
quiz	quizzes

On irregular noun plurals, ▶see **5.11**.

5.10 Adding *-ly* and *-ally*

Many adverbs are formed by adding *-ly* to an adjective:

Adjective	Adverb
quiet	quietly
recent	recently
soft	softly

If the adjective already ends in y, change *y* to *i*:

Adjective	Adverb
steady	steadily
weary	wearily

However, if the adjective ends in *-ic*, add *-ally* (not *-ly*) to form the adverb:

Adjective	Adverb
basic	basically
dramatic	dramatically
enthusiastic	enthusiastically
emphatic	emphatically

genetic	genetically
linguistic	linguistically
realistic	realistically
scientific	scientifically
specific	specifically

The adverb *publicly* (from the adjective *public*) is an exception to this rule.

5.11 Plural nouns

Regular nouns form the plural by adding *-s* to the singular form:

Singular	+ s	= Plural
table	+ s	= tables
truck	+ s	= trucks
elephant	+ s	= elephants

Some plurals are formed by changing the singular ending in an irregular way:

-y → -ies	ability → *abilities*
	memory → *memories*
	party → *parties*
-s → -es	cross → *crosses*
	loss → *losses*
	mass → *masses*

-f or -fe → -ves	thief → *thieves*
	shelf → *shelves*
	life → *lives*
-on → -a	criterion → *criteria*
	phenomenon → *phenomena*
-um → -a	bacterium → *bacteria*
	millennium → *millennia*
-us → -i	focus → *foci*
	nucleus → *nuclei*
-a → -ae	amoeba → *amoebae*
	formula → *formulae*
-o → -oes	echo → *echoes*
	hero → *heroes*
	tomato → *tomatoes*
	But:
	radio → *radios*
	video → *videos*
-is → -es	analysis → *analyses*
	crisis → *crises*
-ex or -ix → -ices	index → *indices*
	matrix → *matrices*

5.12   Variants with *s* or *z*

Many words can be spelled with either *-s-* or *-z-*:

-s- variant	-z- variant
criticise	criticize
finalise	finalize
organise	organize
organisation	organization
polarise	polarize
realise	realize
realisation	realization

Both variants are acceptable, though in general, American English prefers the *-z-* variant, while British English prefers the *-s-* variant.

No choice is available in the following words, which are always spelled with *-s-*:

advise	exercise
arise	guise
chastise	revise
comprise	rise
despise	supervise
disguise	surprise
enterprise	wise

5.13   British and American spelling variants

Spelling differences between British English and American English are not as widespread as is often thought. The vast majority of words have the same spelling in both varieties. However, the following systematic spelling differences may be observed:

	British English	American English
-our / -or	*behaviour*	*behavior*
	colour	*color*
	favourite	*favorite*
	humour	*humor*
	labour	*labor*
	neighbour	*neighbor*
-re / -er	*centre*	*center*
	fibre	*fiber*
	theatre	*theater*
	litre	*liter*
	metre	*meter*
-ogue / -og	*analogue*	*analog*
	catalogue	*catalog*
	dialogue	*dialog*
ae, oe / e	*anaemia*	*anemia*
	anaesthesia	*anesthesia*
	diarrhoea	*diarrhea*
	foetus	*fetus*
	haemorrhage	*hemorrhage*

-ence / -ense	defence	defense
	offence	offense
	pretence	pretense
miscellaneous	aluminium	aluminum
	cheque	check
	jewellery	jewelry
	kerb	curb
	manoeuvre	maneuver
	mould	mold
	plough	plow
	tyre	tire
	sulphur	sulfur

5.14 Problem spellings

Even the most experienced writers have difficulties with the spelling of some words. This is especially true in the case of pairs, like *it's* and *its*, which sound alike but have different spellings and meanings. In this section we disambiguate the most troublesome of these pairs.

accept/except:
Accept is a verb: *You should **accept** his offer. Except* is a preposition (▶see **2.8**): *I like all types of music **except** jazz.*

advice/advise:
Advice is a noun: *Ask your teacher for **advice**. Advise* is a verb: *His doctor **advised** him to stop smoking.*

affect/effect:
Affect is a verb: *Pollution in the atmosphere **affects** our climate. Effect* is a noun: *What **effect** does pollution have? Effect* is sometimes used as a verb, meaning *to bring about (change): The National Health Service has **effected** huge social change in Britain.*

altar/alter:
Altar is a noun: *The sacrifice was placed on the altar.* *Alter* is a verb, meaning *to change*: *It's too late now to alter your holiday plans.*

choose/chose:
Both are forms of the same verb, *choose*. *Choose* is the base form (▶see **2.3.2**): *Choose your clothes carefully, It is difficult to choose.* *Chose* is the past form (▶see **2.3.4**): *We chose a site overlooking the valley.* The *-ed* form of this verb is *chosen*.

council/counsel:
Council is a noun: *The local council has introduced parking restrictions.* *Counsel* is a verb, meaning to guide or advise, usually in relation to behaviour: *We've hired a social worker to counsel the children.* The corresponding noun, *counsel*, means *advice* or *guidance*.

discreet/discrete:
Both are adjectives. *Discreet* means *tactful*: *I've made some discreet enquiries.* The corresponding noun is *discretion*. *Discrete* means *separate, distinct*: *The speech signal is first divided into discrete segments.* The corresponding noun is *discreteness*.

its/it's:
Its is a possessive pronoun (▶see **2.6.2**): *The horse shook its head.* *It's* is a contraction of *it is*: *It's a lovely day* or *it has*: *It's been ages since we met.*

licence/license:
In British English, *licence* is a noun, as in *driving licence*, and *license* is a verb, meaning *to give permission*: *The restaurant is licensed to sell spirits.* *Licence* does not exist in American English. *License* is used as the noun and as the verb.

personal/personnel:
Personal is an adjective: *You shouldn't ask personal questions.* *Personnel* is a noun, meaning *staff*: *All personnel should report to reception.*

practice/practise:

Practice is a noun, meaning (a) training for sport, music, etc: *I've got piano practice at six*, (b) the exercise of a profession, e.g. *medical practice, legal practice*. In British English, *practise* is a verb: *Amy practised her speech in front of a mirror*. The word *practise* does not exist in American English. *Practice* is used as the noun and as the verb.

principal/principle:

Principal is most commonly used as an adjective, meaning *most important*: *The government's principal concern should be unemployment*. As a noun, *principal* refers to the most important, or highest-ranked, person in an organization, e.g. *Principal of a school*. *Principle* is a noun, meaning *rule of conduct*: *a person of principle, moral principles*.

quiet/quite:

Quiet is an adjective: *a quiet child, keep quiet*. *Quite* is an intensifier (▶see **2.5.3**), and is used before an adjective or an adverb: *It's quite cold outside, I spoke to James quite recently*.

stationary/stationery:

Stationary is an adjective: *a stationary vehicle*. *Stationery* is an noun, meaning pens, paper, etc.

than/then:

Than is used in comparative constructions (▶see **4.3.5**): *Paul is older than Amy, The professor is younger than I expected*. *Then* is an adverb of time: *We toured the Museum and then we went home*. As a sentence connector, *then* means *in that case*: *Do you like horror films? Then you'll love Poltergeist*.

your/you're:

Your is a possessive pronoun (▶see **2.6.2**): *Your car has been stolen*. *You're* is a contraction of *you are*: *You're a real pal*.

English irregular verbs

Irregular verbs (▶see **2.3.7**) are verbs in which the past form and the -ed form are not spelled in the regular way. The 'regular way' adds -ed to the base form of the verb (e.g. base form = *walk*, past form = *walked*, -ed form = (has) *walked*). Some of the verbs listed here have regular and irregular variants (▶see **2.3.8**). On the five verb forms, ▶see **2.3.1**. For the verb *be*, ▶see **2.3.9**.

Base form	-s form	Past form	-ed form	-ing form
awake	awakes	awoke	awoken	awaking
bear	bears	bore	borne	bearing
beat	beats	beat	beaten	beating
become	becomes	became	become	becoming
begin	begins	began	begun	beginning
bend	bends	bent	bent	bending
bet	bets	bet	bet	betting
bid	bids	bid	bid	bidding
bind	binds	bound	bound	binding

Base form	-s form	Past form	-ed form	-ing form
bite	bites	bit	bitten	biting
bleed	bleeds	bled	bled	bleeding
blow	blows	blew	blown	blowing
break	breaks	broke	broken	breaking
bring	brings	brought	brought	bringing
breed	breeds	bred	bred	breeding
build	builds	built	built	building
burn	burns	burned	burnt	burning
burst	bursts	burst	burst	bursting
buy	buys	bought	bought	buying
cast	casts	cast	cast	casting
catch	catches	caught	caught	catching
choose	chooses	chose	chosen	choosing
cling	clings	clung	clung	clinging
come	comes	came	come	coming
creep	creeps	crept	crept	creeping
cut	cuts	cut	cut	cutting
deal	deals	dealt	dealt	dealing
dig	digs	dug	dug	digging

Base form	-s form	Past form	-ed form	-ing form
dive	dives	dived	dived	diving
do	does	did	done	doing
draw	draws	drew	drawn	drawing
dream	dreams	dreamed	dreamt	dreaming
drink	drinks	drank	drunk	drinking
drive	drives	drove	driven	driving
eat	eats	ate	eaten	eating
fall	falls	fell	fallen	falling
feed	feeds	fed	fed	feeding
feel	feels	felt	felt	feeling
fight	fights	fought	fought	fighting
find	finds	found	found	finding
flee	flees	fled	fled	fleeing
fling	flings	flung	flung	flinging
fly	flies	flew	flown	flying
forget	forgets	forgot	forgotten	forgetting
freeze	freezes	froze	frozen	freezing
get	gets	got	got	getting
give	gives	gave	given	giving

Base form	-s form	Past form	-ed form	-ing form
go	goes	went	gone	going
grind	grinds	ground	ground	grinding
grow	grows	grew	grown	growing
have	has	had	had	having
hear	hears	heard	heard	hearing
hide	hides	hid	hidden	hiding
hit	hits	hit	hit	hitting
hold	holds	held	held	holding
hurt	hurts	hurt	hurt	hurting
keep	keeps	kept	kept	keeping
kneel	kneels	knelt	knelt	kneeling
knit	knits	knitted	knit	knitting
know	knows	knew	known	knowing
lay	lays	laid	laid	laying
lead	leads	led	led	leading
lean	leans	leaned	leant	leaning
leap	leaps	leaped	leapt	leaping
learn	learns	learned	learnt	learning
leave	leaves	left	left	leaving

Base form	-s form	Past form	-ed form	-ing form
lend	lends	lent	lent	lending
let	lets	let	let	letting
lie[3]	lies	lay	lain	lying
light	lights	lit	lit	lighting
lose	loses	lost	lost	losing
make	makes	made	made	making
mean	means	meant	meant	meaning
meet	meets	met	met	meeting
pay	pays	paid	paid	paying
prove	proves	proved	proven	proving
put	puts	put	put	putting
quit	quits	quit	quit	quitting
read	reads	read	read	reading
ride	rides	rode	ridden	riding
ring	rings	rang	rung	ringing
rise	rises	rose	risen	rising
run	runs	ran	run	running
say	says	said	said	saying

[3] The verb *lie*, meaning *to tell an untruth*, is a regular verb.

Base form	-s form	Past form	-ed form	-ing form
see	sees	saw	seen	seeing
seek	seeks	sought	sought	seeking
sell	sells	sold	sold	selling
send	sends	sent	sent	sending
set	sets	set	set	setting
sew	sews	sewed	sewn	sewing
shake	shakes	shook	shaken	shaking
shine	shines	shone	shone	shining
shoot	shoots	shot	shot	shooting
show	shows	showed	shown	showing
shrink	shrinks	shrank	shrunk	shrinking
shut	shuts	shut	shut	shutting
sing	sings	sang	sung	singing
sink	sinks	sank	sunk	sinking
sit	sits	sat	sat	sitting
sleep	sleeps	slept	slept	sleeping
slide	slides	slid	slid	sliding
smell	smells	smelled	smelt	smelling
speak	speaks	spoke	spoken	speaking

Base form	-s form	Past form	-ed form	-ing form
speed	speeds	sped	sped	speeding
spell	spells	spelled	spelt	spelling
spend	spends	spent	spent	spending
spill	spills	spilled	spilt	spilling
spin	spins	spun	spun	spinning
spit	spits	spat	spat	spitting
split	splits	split	split	splitting
spoil	spoils	spoiled	spoilt	spoiling
spread	spreads	spread	spread	spreading
spring	springs	sprang	sprung	springing
stand	stands	stood	stood	standing
steal	steals	stole	stolen	stealing
stick	sticks	stuck	stuck	sticking
sting	stings	stung	stung	stinging
strike	strikes	struck	struck	striking
string	strings	strung	strung	stringing
strive	strives	strove	striven	striving
swear	swears	swore	sworn	swearing
sweep	sweeps	swept	swept	sweeping

Base form	-s form	Past form	-ed form	-ing form
swell	swells	swelled	swollen	swelling
swim	swims	swam	swum	swimming
swing	swings	swung	swung	swinging
take	takes	took	taken	taking
teach	teaches	taught	taught	teaching
tear	tears	tore	torn	tearing
tell	tells	told	told	telling
think	thinks	thought	thought	thinking
throw	throws	threw	thrown	throwing
wake	wakes	woke	woken	waking
wear	wears	wore	worn	wearing
weave	weaves	wove	woven	weaving
weep	weeps	wept	wept	weeping
win	wins	won	won	winning
wind	winds	wound	wound	winding
wring	wrings	wrung	wrung	wringing
write	writes	wrote	written	writing

Glossary of terms

Acronym

A word formed from the initial letters of other words, e.g. *AIDS* (*acquired immune deficiency syndrome*).

Active

▶See **Voice**.

Adjective

Adjectives express a quality or attribute of a noun: *a happy child; a violent storm; an old car.* Adjectives can also appear after the noun: *the child is happy.*

Adjective phrase

A phrase in which the main word is an adjective. The adjective may occur on its own in the phrase (*happy, old, rich*), or it may have a premodifier before it (*very happy, quite old, extremely rich*). Some adjective phrases may also have postmodifiers after the adjective (*tired of waiting, happy to meet you*).

Adjunct

A grammatically optional element in sentence structure. Adjuncts convey optional, additional information, including when something happened (*Our guests arrived on Sunday.*), where something happened (*We met Paul outside the cinema.*) and why something happened (*Amy cried because she lost her doll.*).

Adjunct clause

A subordinate clause which functions as an adjunct in sentence structure: *Amy cried because she lost her doll; Although he is poor, he gives what he can to charity.*

Adverb

Adverbs are used to modify a verb (*Amy sings **beautifully***), an adjective (***extremely** big*), or another adverb (***very** recently*).

Adverb phrase

A phrase in which the main word is an adverb. The adverb may occur on its own (*beautifully, recently*), or it may have a premodifier before it (*very **beautifully**, quite **recently***).

Alternative interrogative

A question which offers two or more alternative responses: *Do you want tea or coffee?*; *Is that William or Harry?* Cf.: **Yes–no interrogative**.

Anaphora

The use of a word or words to refer back to something previously mentioned. The personal pronouns are often used anaphorically, as in *James likes football. **He** never misses a game*. Here, *he* refers anaphorically to *James*. Cf.: **Cataphora**.

Antecedent

A word or words to which a following word refers back. In *James likes football. He never misses a game*, *James* is the antecedent of *he*. Cf.: **Anaphora, Cataphora**.

Apposition

A relationship between two units (usually noun phrases), in which both units refer to the same person or thing: *The President, Mr Brown*.

Article

The articles are *the* (the definite article) and *a/an* (the indefinite article).

Aspect

Aspect expresses how an event is viewed with respect to time. There are two aspects in English, the progressive aspect (*William is leaving/was leaving*) and the perfective aspect (*William has left/had left*).

Asyndetic coordination

Coordination without the use of *and*: *We need **bread, cheese, eggs, milk, flour***. Cf.: **Syndetic coordination, Polysyndetic coordination**.

Auxiliary verb

A 'helping' verb which typically comes before the main verb in a sentence

(I can drive; James has written to the Council.). Auxiliary verbs are divided into the following types: modal, passive, progressive, perfective, *do* auxiliary, semi-auxiliary.

Back formation
A verb formed by removing a noun ending, and adding a verb ending, e.g. *televise*, from *television*.

Base form
The form of a verb which follows *to*, and to which the inflections are added: *to walk, walk+s, walk+ed, walk+ing*.

Case
A distinction chiefly in pronouns which relates to their grammatical functions. Personal pronouns and the pronoun *who* have two cases: subjective case (e.g. *I, we, who*) and objective case (*me, us, whom*). Nouns exhibit two cases, the common case (*dog, dogs*) and the genitive case (*dog's, dogs'*).

Cataphora
The use of a word or words to refer forward to a later word: *When you see him, will you ask Simon to phone me?* Cf.: **Anaphora**.

Clause
A sentence-like construction which operates at a level lower than a sentence.

Cleft sentence
A sentence with the pattern *It* + *be* + focus + relative clause, e.g. *It was William who noticed the error.* (cf. *William noticed the error.*). Cleft sentences are used to emphasize the focus, here, *William*.

Clipping
A type of abbreviation in which one or more syllables are omitted from a word, e.g. *demo*, from *demonstration*.

Comment clause
A peripheral clause in sentence structure, used to offer a comment on what is being said: *I can't afford it, I'm afraid.*

Comparative clause
Comparative clauses are introduced by *than*, and express comparison: *The play was better than I expected; David is stronger than he used to be.*

Complement

A unit which completes the meaning of a word, e.g., a noun (*the fact that the earth is round*), or a preposition (*under the table*). The term is also applied to the unit which completes the meaning of a transitive verb (*The soldiers destroyed **the village**.*).

Complex sentence

A sentence which contains one or more subordinate clauses: *The match was abandoned **because the pitch was waterlogged***; *The referee decided **to abandon the match***.

Compound sentence

A sentence which consists of two or more clauses linked by a coordinating conjunction (*and, but, or*): *Emily works during the day **and** she studies at night.*

Concord

Another term for **subject–verb agreement**.

Conditional clause

A conditional clause is typically introduced by *if*, and expresses a condition: ***If we get home early** we can watch the new video.*

Conjunction

The coordinating conjunctions (*and, but, or*) link elements of equal status (*I play guitar **and** David sings.*). The subordinating conjunctions (e.g. *if, because, since*) introduce a subordinate clause: (*Have some pasta **if** you want it.*).

Coordination

The linking of two or more units using one of the coordinating conjunctions *and, but* and *or*: *We bought meat **and** vegetables*; *David graduated last year **but** he still can't find a job*; *You don't need money **or** good looks.*

Copular verb

Another term for **linking verb**.

Countable noun

Countable nouns denote things that can be counted: *one chair, two chairs, three chairs*, etc. Therefore they have both a singular form (*chair*) and a plural form (*chairs*). Also called count nouns. Cf.: **Uncountable noun.**

Declarative sentence

A sentence which is chiefly used for making a statement: *The sky was blue*; *William became an engineer*; *The government has a huge majority*. Cf.: **Interrogative sentence**.

Definite article

The definite article is the word *the*.

Demonstrative pronoun

The demonstrative pronouns are *this*, *that*, *these* and *those*.

Determiner

Determiners are elements in the structure of a noun phrase. They introduce the noun phrase: *the computer*; *a newspaper*; *some people*; *many problems*; *three ships*; *all our friends*.

Direct object

The element required by a transitive verb to complete its meaning: *David announced his retirement*; *The company made a huge profit*. Direct objects are most commonly noun phrases, but they can also be clauses: *David announced that he will retire*.

Direct speech

A method of reporting speech in which the actual words that were used are quoted: *'I'm very tired', said James*. Cf.: **Indirect speech**.

Do auxiliary

The *do* auxiliary is used (a) to form questions (*Do you like French films?*) (b) to form negatives, with *not* (*I do not enjoy violent films.*), (c) to form negative directives, with *not* (*Do not sit there!*) (d) for emphasis (*I do enjoy a good book!*).

Etymology

The study of the origin and history of words.

Exclamative sentence

A sentence that expresses an exclamation: *What a pity!*; *How tall he's grown!*

Existential sentence

▶See *There-sentence*.

Finite

If the first (or only) verb in a verb phrase exhibits tense (past or present), then the verb phrase is finite. The following sentences all contain a finite verb phrase: *David left early*; *David leaves at eight every morning*; *David is leaving now*; *David had left*. The term is also applied to clauses in which the verb phrase is finite. Cf.: **Non-finite**.

Form

In grammatical descriptions, the term *form* refers to the structure, appearance, or 'shape' of an element. For instance, we say that the adjective *old* has three forms, *old, older, oldest*. Cf.: **Function**.

Fragment

An incomplete sentence, often used in response to a question: *Where did you leave the keys? On the table*. Fragments are interpreted as complete sentences: *I left the keys on the table*. Cf.: **Non-sentence**.

Function

The grammatical role that an element performs in a sentence, clause, or phrase. For instance, in *The old man is ill*, the element *the old man* (a noun phrase) performs the function of subject. In turn, the adjective *old* performs the function of premodifier in the noun phrase *the old man*. Cf.: **Form**.

Gradable

A term used to describe adjectives and adverbs which can be modified by an intensifier: *fairly cold*; *very cold*; *extremely cold*, and have comparative and superlative forms: *old, older, oldest*.

Imperative sentence

A type of sentence used in giving orders: *Move over, Come in, Don't leave your coat there*.

Indefinite article

The indefinite article is *a/an*.

Indirect object

Some transitive verbs require two elements to complete their meaning: *We gave James a gift*. Here, *James* is the indirect object, and *a gift* is the direct object. The indirect object typically refers to the person who receives something or benefits from the action.

Indirect speech

Indirect speech reports what has been said, but not in the actual words used by the speaker: *James said that he was very tired*. Compare: *'I'm very tired', said James*, which is **direct speech**.

Infinitive

The base form of a verb when it is introduced by *to*: *She loves **to sing**; They decided **to cooperate***.

Inflection

An ending which indicates a grammatical category. For instance, the *-s* ending added to a noun indicates plural number.

Intensifier

A type of adverb used to express degree in an adjective or in another adverb. The most common intensifier is *very*: ***very** cold*; ***very** recently*. Other intensifiers include *extremely, fairly, highly, quite*.

Interrogative sentence

A type of sentence used in asking questions: *Is James here? Did you have a good time? What is this? How is the patient?*

Intransitive verb

A verb which requires no other element to complete its meaning: *David yawned; It is still snowing*. Cf.: **Transitive verb**.

Linking verb

The most common linking verb is *be*: *My uncle **is** a professional footballer*. Linking verbs link the subject (*my uncle*) with the subject complement (*a professional footballer*). Other linking verbs include *seem* (*He **seems** angry.*) and *appear* (*She **appears** distracted.*).

Main clause

A clause which can stand independently. In *Emily worked in Greece when she was young*, the main clause is *Emily worked in Greece*. The second clause, *when she was young*, can be omitted, and is a subordinate clause.

Main verb

In the verb phrase *was raining*, *raining* is the main verb, while *was* is the auxiliary verb.

Mass noun
Another term for **uncountable noun**.

Modal auxiliary
The modal auxiliary verbs are *can, could, may, might, must, shall, should, will, would*.

Mood
A grammatical category which indicates the attitude of the speaker to what is said. English has three moods: indicative, imperative, subjunctive.

Morphology
The study of the structure of words.

Multi-word verb
A combination consisting of a verb and one or two other words, acting as a unit. Multi-word verbs include prepositional verbs (*look at, rely on*), phrasal verbs (*give in, take over*), and phrasal-prepositional verbs (*look forward to, put up with*).

Nominal relative clause
A subordinate clause introduced by *what, whatever, whoever, where*: **What you need** is a long holiday; I can't understand **what he is saying**; I'll speak to **whoever is responsible**.

Non-finite
If the first (or only) verb in a verb phrase has the base form (S*imon is reluctant **to make an effort**.*), the *-ing* form (***Working hard** brings its own reward.*) or the *-ed* form (***Published in 1998**, it soon became a best-seller.*), then the verb phrase is non-finite. The term is also used to describe a clause containing a non-finite verb phrase. Cf.: **Finite**.

Non-restrictive relative
A 'non-defining' relative clause, which simply adds information: *The passenger, **who was about 20**, was not injured.* Compare the 'defining' restrictive relative clause: *The passenger **who was in the rear seat** was not injured.*

Non-sentence
An independent unit which has no sentence structure. Non-sentences are commonly used in public signs and notices: *Exit, No Entry, 10% Off.* Cf.: **Fragment**.

Noun

Common nouns are the names of objects (*book, computer*), people (*boy, father*), states (*loneliness, happiness*), abstract concepts (*history, honesty*), etc. Proper nouns refer to individual people (*Nelson Mandela, Winston Churchill*), places (*London, Hong Kong*), and geographical features (*Ben Nevis, River Thames*).

Noun phrase

A phrase in which the main word is a noun. The noun may occur on its own (*children,* water), or it may have a premodifier before it (*young children, cold water*). A noun phrase may also contain a postmodifier after the noun (**children** *with learning disabilities,* **cold water** *from the stream*). A noun phrase may be introduced by a determiner (**the** *children,* **some** *water*).

Number contrast

The contrast between singular and plural, e.g. *dog/dogs, woman/women, this/these.*

Object

▶See **Direct object**, **Indirect object**.

Object complement

A sentence element which denotes an attribute of the object. For instance, in *The dye turned the water blue, blue* denotes the colour of *the water* (the object), so *blue* is the object complement.

Objective case

The objective case of a personal pronoun is used when the pronoun is a direct object (*Simon met* **me.**) or an indirect object (*Simon bought* **me** *a ticket.*). It is also used after a preposition (*Simon bought a ticket for* **me.**). Cf.: **Subjective case.**

Parenthetical

A complete sentence inserted in another sentence: *The merger –* **this is** **confidential** *– will go ahead as planned.*

Participial adjective

An adjective with an *-ed* ending (*a* **dedicated** *worker*) or an *-ing* ending (*a* **surprising** *result*).

Participle
The *-ed* and *-ing* forms of a verb. In some grammars, these are called the *-ed* participle (or past participle) and the *-ing* participle (or present participle).

Passive
▶See **Voice**.

Perfective auxiliary
The perfective auxiliary is *have*. It occurs before the *-ed* form of a main verb: *Simon **has** arrived*; *We **had** hoped you could come.*

Personal pronoun
The personal pronouns are *I/me, you, he/him, she/her, it, we/us, they/them.*
▶See **Subjective case**, **Objective case**.

Phrasal verb
▶See **Multi-word verb**.

Phrasal-prepositional verb
▶See **Multi-word verb**.

Polysyndetic coordination
Coordination in which *and* or *or* is used between each pair of co-ordinated items: *The lecture went on **and** on **and** on*; *You can have pasta **or** meatloaf **or** salad.* Cf.: **Asyndetic coordination, Syndetic coordination**.

Possessive pronoun
The possessive pronouns are *my/mine, your/yours, his, her/hers, its, our/ours, their/theirs.*

Predicate
Everything in a sentence excluding the subject: *David* (subject) *won a scholarship* (predicate).

Prefix
A sequence of letters, such as *un-* (*unlawful*), *anti-* (*anti-abortion*), *post-* (*post-war*) added to the beginning of a word to form a new word. Cf.: **Suffix**.

Preposition

Common prepositions include *after, at, before, beside, for, in, of, under, with*. Prepositions are used to introduce a noun phrase: *after the ballet*; *at the supermarket*; *before breakfast*.

Prepositional complement

The element (usually a noun phrase) which is introduced by a preposition: *after **the ballet**; under **our roof**, in **New York**, at **ten o'clock***.

Prepositional phrase

A phrase which is introduced by a preposition. The preposition is followed by a prepositional complement, which is usually a noun phrase: *after the ballet*; *under our roof*; *in New York*; *at ten o'clock*.

Prepositional verb

▶See **Multi-word verb**.

Progressive auxiliary

The progressive auxiliary *be* occurs before a main verb with *-ing* form: *I **am** organising a trip to Paris*; *Paul **is** collecting money for charity*; *The children **were** shouting*.

Pronoun

Pronouns are divided into the following main classes: **demonstrative, personal, possessive, reflexive**.

Reduced relative clause

A relative clause in which the relative pronoun is omitted, and the verb has *-ed* form or *-ing* form: *Films **produced on a small budget** are rarely successful* (compare: *Films **which are produced on a small budget***); *The man **standing beside you** is my uncle* (compare: *The man **who is standing beside you***).

Reflexive pronoun

The reflexive pronouns are *myself, yourself, himself, herself, itself, ourselves, yourselves, themselves*.

Relative clause

A relative clause is introduced by a relative pronoun such as *who, which*, or *that*: *The man **who lives beside us** is unwell*; *It's a new company **which specializes in web design***; *The project **that I'm working on** is really interesting*.

Relative pronoun
The relative pronouns are *who(m)*, *whose*, *which*, and *that*. They are used to introduce a relative clause: *The man **who lives beside us** is unwell.*

Reporting clause
A clause such as *he said*, or *said Mary*, which identifies the speaker of direct speech: *'I'm leaving now,' **he said**.*

Restrictive relative clause
A defining relative clause, which identifies the noun preceding it: *The passenger **who was in the rear seat** was not injured.* Cf.: **Non-restrictive relative clause**.

Semantics
The study of the relationship between linguistic forms and meaning.

Semi-auxiliary
A multi-word auxiliary verb. Examples include *have to* (*I **had to** catch a bus.*), *be going to* (*He's **going to** fall.*) and *be about to* (*The factory **is about to** close.*).

Sentential relative clause
A relative clause which expresses a comment on what has previously been said: *Amy can't come this evening, **which is a pity**.*

Simple sentence
A sentence which contains no subordinate clause.

Subject
The sentence element that typically comes before the verb in a declarative sentence: ***James** (S) is (V) still at school.* In an interrogative sentence, the subject and the verb change places with each other: *Is (V) **James** (S) still at school?*

Subject complement
The sentence element that completes the meaning of a linking verb (usually *be*): *Paul **is my nephew**; Our house **is too small**; The weather **was beautiful**.*

Subjective case

The subjective case of a personal pronoun is used when the pronoun acts as subject: *I met Simon,* in contrast with the objective case: *Simon met me.*

Subject–verb agreement

A term used to denote the fact that a verb form agrees in number (singular or plural) with its subject (compare: *The dog barks./The dogs bark.*). Subject–verb agreement applies only to present tense verbs. Also known as **concord**.

Subjunctive

A term used to denote sentences which express a hypothetical or non-factual situation: *If I were you, I would invest the money*; *The Report recommended that the police officers be suspended immediately.*

Subordinate clause

A dependent clause within a larger structure (*John said that Mary is leaving.*). Here, the subordinate clause is introduced by the subordinating conjunction *that.*

Subordinating conjunction

A word which introduces a subordinate clause. Common subordinating conjunctions include: *although, because, if, since, that, when, while.* Multi-word subordinating conjunctions include *as long as, as though, provided that, rather than.*

Subordination

A relationship between two clauses in which one clause is grammatically dependent on the other. Subordination is often overtly indicated by the use of a subordinating conjunction: *William studied architecture while he was in Germany.*

Suffix

An ending added to a word to create another word. Noun suffixes include *-ness* (*coolness, kindness*), and *-ism* (*capitalism, optimism*). Adjective suffixes include *-able* (*profitable, reasonable*) and *-al* (*accidental, musical*).

Syndetic coordination

Coordination using *and, but,* or *or*: *Paul and Amy*; *tired but happy*; *tea or coffee.* Cf.: **Asyndetic coordination, Polysyndetic coordination**.

Syntax
The study of the arrangement of words in a sentence.

Tag question
A question which is appended to a statement: *You went to Harvard, didn't you?*; *You're not leaving, are you?*

Tense
There are two tenses in English: the past tense and the present tense. Tense is denoted by the form of the verb: *David **walks** to school* (present tense); *David **walked** to school* (past tense).

***That*-clause**
A subordinate clause introduced by the subordinating conjunction *that*: *Everyone knows **that smoking is dangerous**.*

***There*-sentence**
A sentence introduced by *there*, followed, usually, by the verb *be*: ***There is a fly in my soup**; **There is something wrong with the printer***. Also called an **existential sentence**.

Transitive verb
A verb which requires another element to complete its meaning: *Paul **makes** model airplanes*; *David **bought** a boat*. Cf.: **Intransitive verb**.

Uncountable noun
A noun which denotes things which are considered as indivisible wholes (*furniture, mud, software*) and therefore cannot be counted (**two furnitures, *three muds, *four softwares*, etc.). Uncountable nouns have a singular form (*software*), but no plural form (**softwares*). Cf.: **Countable noun**.

Verb
Verbs are divided into two types: (a) main verbs, such as *break, buy, eat, sing, write* and (b) auxiliary verbs such as *can, could, may, must, might, shall, should, will, would*.

Verb phrase
A phrase in which the main word is a verb. The verb may occur on its own (*walked, sings*), or it may be preceded by one or more auxiliary verbs (*has walked, can walk, has been singing*).

Verbless clause

A subordinate clause which lacks a main verb: *Though poor, he gives what he can to charity.* (cf. *Though he is poor* ...).

Voice

A term used to describe the contrast between an active sentence: *The police arrested the suspect*; and a passive sentence: *The suspect was arrested (by the police).*

Wh-interrogative

A question introduced by *who, what, where, when* or *how*: *Who was at the door?*; *What would you like to drink?*; *Where are my keys?*; *When is your flight?*; *How do you switch it on?*

Yes–no interrogative

A question which normally expects an answer which is either *yes* or *no*: *Did you enjoy the film?* – *Yes/No.* Cf.: **Alternative interrogative**.

Zero relative clause

A relative clause which is not introduced by a relative pronoun: *This is the book **William recommended**.* Cf.: *This is the book **that** William recommended.*

Zero subordinate clause

A subordinate clause from which the subordinating conjunction *that* has been omitted: *He **must think I'm a fool**.* Cf.: *He **must think that I'm a fool**.*

Further reading

Chalker, Sylvia and Edmund Weiner (1994) *The Oxford Dictionary of English Grammar*, Oxford: Clarendon Press.

Collins, Peter (1999) *English Grammar*, London: Longman.

Crystal, David (1995) *The Cambridge Encyclopedia of the English Language*, Cambridge: Cambridge University Press.

Crystal, David (1996) *Rediscover Grammar*, 2nd edn, London: Longman.

Greenbaum, Sidney (1990) *An Introduction to English Grammar*, London: Longman.

Greenbaum, Sidney (1996) *The Oxford English Grammar*, Oxford: Oxford University Press.

Greenbaum, Sidney (2000) *The Oxford Reference Grammar*, Oxford: Oxford University Press.

Greenbaum, Sidney and Janet Whitcut (1988) *Guide to English Usage*, London: Longman.

Hughes, Anthony (1996) *Online English Grammar*, Digital Education Network Ltd. (http://www.edunet.com/english/grammar/index.cfm)

Hurford, James (1994) *Grammar: A Student's Guide*, Cambridge: Cambridge University Press.

Nelson, Gerald and Justin Buckley (1998) *The Internet Grammar of English*, Survey of English Usage, University College London. (http://www.ucl.ac.uk/internet-grammar/).

Trask, R. L. (1993) *A Dictionary of Grammatical Terms in Linguistics*, London and New York: Routledge.

Index

a 75
abbreviation 133
acronym 133
active sentence 21, 70
adjective 48
adjective phrase 95
adjunct 22
adjunct clause 104
adjunct clause meanings
    109
adjunct meanings 23
adverb 53
adverb meanings 56
adverb phrase 97
agentless passive 21
agreement 11
alternative interrogative 26
American spelling 6, 146
an 75
anaphora 120
antecedent 120
antecedent agreement 121
apostrophe 36
apposition 85
article 75
aspect 92
asyndetic coordination 114
auxiliary verb 39, 88

back formation 135
bad 51
base form 40
be 13, 46, 70

blending 132
British and American spelling 4, 146

cardinal numeral 76
case 59
cataphora 121
clause 10, 102ff.
cleft sentence 124
clipping 135
closed word class 30
combining form 136
comment clause 111
common noun 34
comparative adjective 50
comparative adverb 55
comparative clause 107
complement 84
complex sentence 10, 101
compound sentence 9
compounding 130
conjunction 73
connector 116
coordinating conjunction 73
coordination 113ff
countable noun 35, 75

declarative sentence 25
definite article 75
demonstrative pronoun 63
dependent genitive 37
dependent possessive pronoun 60
determiner 80
direct object 16

direct speech 111
do 71, 122

-ed clause 103
-ed form 42
either . . . or 74
exclamative sentence 27

fast 53
finite verb phrase 91, 103
fragment 27
fronting 123
future time 90

gender 38, 59
gender-neutral pronoun 62
genitive noun 36
get 70
good 51
gradable adjective 49
gradable adverb 54
grammar 1
grammar rules 1
grammatical hierarchy 7

hard 53
have 70
helping verb 67

imperative sentence 26, 93
indefinite article 75
independent genitive 37
independent possessive pronoun 61
indicative mood 93
indirect object 17
indirect speech 111
infinitive 40
inflection 40, 137,
-ing clause 103
-ing form 43
intensifier 55
International Corpus of English 7
interrogative sentence 25
intransitive verb 12

inversion 11
irregular verb 43, 150
it 65, 124, 125
it's 148
its 61, 148

linking verb 13
logical connector 116
-ly adverb 53, 142

main verb 39
mandative subjunctive 94
modal auxiliary 68
modal auxiliary meanings 69
mood 93
more 50, 55
most 50, 55
multi-word preposition 73
multi-word subordinator 74
multi-word verb 47

neither . . . nor 74
nominal relative clause 105
non-finite clause 103
non-finite verb phrase 91
non-sentence 28
nonrestrictive postmodifier 84
not 122
noun 32
noun phrase 79
number contrast 33
numeral 76

object complement 18
objective case 59
one 66
open word class 30
ordinal numeral 76

parenthetical 112
participial adjective 52
passive auxiliary 70
passive sentence 21, 70
past form 41

perfective aspect 93
perfective auxiliary 70
peripheral clause 110
personal pronoun 57
phrasal verb 47
phrasal-prepositional verb 48
phrase 79
phrase types 78
plural noun 32, 143
polysyndetic coordination 114
possessive pronoun 60
postmodifier 83
postponed subject 125
predicate 10
prefix 127
premodifier 82
preposition 72
prepositional complement 98
prepositional phrase 98
prepositional verb 47
progressive aspect 92
progressive auxiliary 70
pronoun 57
proper noun 34
pseudo-coordination 115

reduced relative clause 105
referring expression 120
reflexive pronoun 62
relative clause 105
relative pronoun 64
reporting clause 111
restrictive postmodifier 84

-s form 41
semi-auxiliary 72
sentence 9
sentence patterns 19
sentential relative 113
shall 69
simple sentence 9
singular noun 32

so 122
spelling rules 138ff
spelling variants 145ff
standard English 2
structural connector 117
subject 10
subject complement 15
subjective case 59
subjunctive mood 94
subordinate clause 102
subordinating conjunction 74, 102
subordination 101
suffix 129
superlative adjective 50
superlative adverb 55
syndetic coordination 114

tag question 112
tense 89
that 103, 105
that-clause 106
there sentence 126
to-clause 103
transitive verb 14

uncountable noun 35, 76

verb 11, 39
verb forms 39ff.
verb phrase 88
vocative 24
voice 22

were-subjunctive 94
wh-interrogative 26
who 64
whom 64
will 68, 90
word classes 30
world English 3

zero relative clause 105